The Story of
Christina and I

A Real-Life Urban Fairy Tale
An Inspirational Collaborative Memoir

Christina S. Sledge and Edward L. Sledge Jr.

Sledge House
Media

CHRISTINA & EDWARD SLEDGE

ISBN 978-0-578-92959-0
Library of Congress Control Number 2021905236
Independently published in the United States by
Sledge House Media

Front and back cover design by Hampton
Lamoureux TS95 Studios
Back cover photo by Trene Forbes

Dedication

First, we give all praise and glory to *God* and *Jesus Christ* our *Lord* and Personal Savior.

Second, our book is dedicated to our beautiful daughters because they give us joy, laughter, and love.

From Eddie…

To my father. I became the man we both could not even imagine. You always pulled me back from any long and dark road I was on or was heading to, and I miss you every day. Writing this book, I embraced you even more and truly understand what you were doing for me.

From Christina…

To Mama. Thank you for being my guiding light and constant positive motivation, encouraging me to do my best, and teaching me that anything is possible.

To my parents. Mommy, thank you for raising me and teaching me to embrace the fun and enjoyable parts of life. Daddy, thank you for stepping up to be my father, teaching me work ethic and hustle. Thank you both for being my supporters.

From Both of Us...

To Shamean and David. Both of you inspire us to become nothing less than successful. It brings us joy to know we have made both of you proud since you both are our standard of success.

We were blessed to encounter so many great people before and during our marriage, and we are grateful for all of them. Therefore, we say thank you to Brandon M., Rolando S., Christina B., Addie G., Dorne E., Brianna M., Cory B., Mike G., Dr. Baria J., Ebony B., Natasha C., Quori Tyler B., TJ and Tony K., Andre G., Tyrone D., Sallie M., Kayla J. Chi B., Doreen B., Kenny and Dawn R., Richard J., Lynn B., Richard and Ebony G., Nikki and Alphie W., Debra T., Shannon and Jarrad D., Joe M., Steve and Darlene B., Willie L., and Lori and Charlie P, Sheryl B. our nieces, nephews, friends, our extended family, and our first customer Shawn G. Smith.

In loving memory of Enid K. Durant, Edward L. Sledge Sr., Antonio "Powerful" M., Kena V., Ellen B., Elton C., George C., Brenda D., James and Sadie G., Clarence G., Wayne G., Choicey J., Sophia Sledge, Melo Sledge, Francis V. S., and Marilyn W.

Finally, thank you to everyone who supported us and purchased our book.

Foreword

My husband is my best friend and soulmate. We met when we were fourteen years old, and he has been a major part of my life ever since. I can't imagine what my life would have been like without him. The most amazing thing about Eddie is his selflessness. Although he is considered boisterous by some, Eddie is very humble when it comes to the many selfless acts he has performed for others. He once received a medal for helping a family from their burning home when he was a soldier in the U.S. Army. He considers it an honor to donate blood since he became a blood donor with the Red Cross in 2002.

I consider it an honor to be married to my husband. He continues to astound me with his ability to see the bright side of any situation. Throughout our twenty-one years of marriage, he continues to be optimistic with the thought that life will be better especially whenever we encounter obstacles. I learned how to be resilient from Eddie because he experienced so much trauma at a young age, a fire in his house, homelessness, his stepmother's serious illness, and the death of both his parents by the time he was twenty-two. Eddie has also been an extraordinary husband and friend to me throughout our marriage. He taught me how to drive and helped me obtain my driver's license. He has been there with me through job losses, bad bosses, health issues, deaths in our family, celebrations, and my own accomplishments. I see his accomplishments and they inspire me to continue to do more.

When we were newlyweds, he always joked that he would take me places and he did that and more. Not only did we have the opportunity to visit many places and experience wonderful things together, he took me places with the different perspective that he brings to the world and people. Every time, he comes home from work, he has an interesting story to share about the people that crossed his path that day. I am extremely proud of the man Edward has become over the last twenty-one years. I have witnessed him evolve from a teenage boy from Brooklyn to a husband and father, a master's graduate, and the list continues to grow. At our fifteenth year vow renewal, one of our best men, Rich called us a power couple. I never thought of us that way until I reflect on where we started and what we accomplished. Many of our accomplishments are attributed to the tenacity, ambition, and drive that Eddie puts forth every day. We became a power couple because we make each other stronger. Thank you, Eddie, I love you with all my heart.

Christina S. Sledge

Introduction

Why did we select the title *The Story of Christina and I*? I created the title to convey the importance of Christina in my life. Even Christina pleaded with me to change the title, and our book editor told us it was grammatically incorrect and that we should change the title to The Story of Christina and Eddie. Although our book is written from both points of view, I wanted to emphasize how my wife changed my life. Anyone who knows us understands that I am not afraid to share with the world the love I have for Christina. Therefore, it is only natural that I continue placing the highest praise I can on her. I learned that I was meant to be her husband, and she was meant to be my wife. The same amount of times we could have met or continue dating before we married, is equal to the times I faced death before we married. I truly believe the *Lord* was saving me for her.

From teenagers holding hands riding the L train in Brooklyn to married adults holding hands while driving in one of our luxury cars, Christina (Chris) and I (Eddie) made it! We have been married for twenty-one wonderful years; however, we have known each other for twenty-eight years. From the moment we finished saying "I do" to each other and after our first kiss as a married couple, we only had fifty cents. I called my father and told him that we just got married, and he and his girlfriend, Eleanor, wired fifty dollars to us as a congratulations gift. At the time, I was a soldier in the army stationed in Georgia with a 1991 black Chrysler New Yorker with over 175,000 miles and making only $22,000 per year, and Chris was a senior at Temple University and was soon to be evicted from her apartment in Philadelphia. She moved in with one of her college friends, sleeping on her couch for a few months trying to finish college, and I rented us a two-story townhome in a nice quiet neighborhood ten minutes from base. However, we didn't live together until she came down for Thanksgiving in 2000 while she was pregnant with our first daughter. We had food, but we didn't have any money for anything else. Once in a while we ate at an all-you-can-eat buffet restaurant called the Western Sizzlin, we rented videos from Blockbuster, we used bedsheets as curtains, and we had a nineteen-inch television without cable. Our neighbors' parents (who were veterans) gave us four single mattresses, and we pushed them together making our first bed.

It is amazing how we overcame our early struggles to get to where we are today, and although it has not been an easy, but it has been a terrific fairy tale. In our marriage, we only depend on ourselves because we didn't want anyone interfering in our relationship. We came from having only two quarters and one old car, living in a military town, and without any degrees, to four degrees, luxury cars, and living in a city once voted one of the best places to live in America. We give *God* and *Jesus Christ* all the praise and glory because we were (and still are) blessed as we turned nothing into something.

Our book is not a blueprint of how to stay together in a marriage or the secrets of staying in love, but it is a celebration of our successful marriage. It shares the heartaches, blessings, and experiences of our lives and our twenty-one years of marriage. Our book expresses the highs and lows of our friendship as parents, partners, and best friends, and it also discusses the relationships we have with our families and friends along our journey. Also, it explains key moments, life-changing experiences, and how we were meant to be together regardless of the differences in our upbringing, teenage years, and early adulthoods. Our book is broken into three parts. The first part discusses our individual lives from birth to the beginning of high school, the second part discusses our lives when we met in high school until the end of our first year of marriage, and the third part discusses key aspects of our twenty-one years of marriage.

Chris and I have many things in common. We were born in the same hospital (which my father and her grandmother worked at without knowing each other), born out of wedlock, have stepfamilies, are considered old souls since we were reared by close relatives who were our elders, are alphas that are super focused on our goals, and are inspired by someone we admired who lived in Maryland. However, we also have some differences. Although we both are highly educated with master's degrees, there is no doubt Chris is the brains of our operation, and I provide the muscle and the patience. She aims extremely high because she was raised to have high expectations, and I am content with living simply as long as there aren't any major issues. Chris was raised around positive role models who taught her she could do whatever she wanted to do in her life. Therefore, she doesn't have any patience because she expects things to occur on her timetable without any issues. On the other hand, I did not grow up with positive role models, and they taught me about surviving the streets, to never trust anyone, and the world is not made of marshmallows. No matter the situation Chris and I faced, be it moving, planning, finding employment, parenting, or even family events, she was always thinking about the next steps and the risks. However, I am a realist and tend to not worry about things because I am the "just tell me the time and place and I got you" type of person. She is an optimist and idealist. She loves inspiring stories and movies with happy endings especially Hallmark movies, and I enjoy documentaries about drugs and dysfunctional families.

Our story includes so many people; however, only four (willingly and unwillingly) played significant roles connecting Chris and me together. Chris's father, Alfredo, unknowingly set up the dots for Chris and me to meet, and because of her brother Antonio (Tony, later known as Powerful) and her mother, Lisa, Chris and I stayed connected even when we dated other people, and my father, Big Eddie purposely orchestrated our marriage proposal and subsequently our engagement. Chris and I believe that *God* and *Jesus Christ* always wanted us together. Our story reads like it came out of *The Adjustment Bureau* or *The Notebook*.

We believe we manifested each other because she prayed for a good man to enter her life, and I wished for a good woman I could love mentally and physically. I was meant to be in her life for emotional support, and she was meant to be in my life to provide me peace. During our teenage and young adult years, there were opportunities when we could have started dating again; however, we didn't because we had to live our lives separately before becoming a committed couple. We believe we had to experience painful and exhausting relationships with other people, so that we could learn we weren't missing out on anyone or anything. Chris is awesome! From high school and throughout our marriage, the things I loved about her I still do plus more. She is intelligent, she has passion for what she is interested in, she is determined to find the root cause of an issue, she is a leader, and she has her own style because she receives compliments from other women almost everywhere we go. It's crazy that I still give her butterflies, and I cannot stop touching her. I am her Pepé Le Pew and she is my Penelope.

There are so many places and events we have been blessed to have experienced. We have traveled to many cities and been to Canada. We have visited Universal Studios, the Statue of Liberty, and Niagara Falls, we have stood on top of four of the five tallest buildings in the world, and we have participated in cancer walks. We have seen concerts performed by our favorite R&B and hip-hop artists, and we have even gone to an opera. We have been on the jumbotron during the kiss cam at an NBA basketball game, and to top it off, we had a Disney Fairy Tale wedding.

How to Read This Book

This book is written from the first-person perspective. Each chapter is told from either Eddie or Christina's perspective. We recommend reading the chapters as if you are Eddie or Christina. You will be taken on the journey from both points of view (POV). It is a unique take on a memoir that allows the reader to learn both sides of the story.

Part One: Eddie And Christina

Little Eddie
(1977–1992)—Eddie's POV

I was born in 1977, in Kings County Hospital in Brooklyn, NY, to a young married mother named Marilyn and her much older boyfriend, Edward "Big Eddie." My mother (who was almost twenty years younger than my father) died when I was six months old and three days after she attempted suicide while she was holding me sitting in front of an open window. She suddenly leaned forward, and my father saw her and tried to grab both of us, but she slipped through his hands. My mother's family was from Barbados, and she was one of six children, which included five daughters; however, she was labeled the "black sheep" of her family. Her parents (my grand- mother Marie and my grandfather Clarence, both of whom I never met) were married. Clarence was a strict, church-devoted black man, and Marie was 100 percent Bajan. They divorced, and Clarence soon married a woman named Addie (I have known her as my only grandmother). In fact, Clarence and Big Eddie were friends, since Big Eddie worked with my Uncle Charlie (who was married to Addie's sister), and Clarence introduced Big Eddie to Marilyn while she was married for several years to a Bajan man. I don't know why they were separated, but Big Eddie and Marilyn lived together shortly before I was born.

My mother was an extremely well-dressed woman and an excellent cook; however, she was mentally ill, and her illness became worse after giving birth to me because she was schizophrenic. I was told that she couldn't stay in one place because she moved around a lot as if she were always on the run. There were times when she called her father late at night to come pick her up from unfamiliar locations, and he and her youngest brother, Clarence Jr. (who was a preteen), both would go get her, but then she would be gone and call them again from another place. To cope with her illness and attempt to stay calm, she normally used cocaine with Big Eddie while and after being pregnant with me. She may have been on cocaine during the time she attempted suicide with me in her arms, and that her cocaine use may be the reason I am a loud talker and always moving too fast. Big Eddie told me that before she died, he promised my mother that he wouldn't let her family take me away from him, and he stated that he fought to the bitter end to keep me. I don't know why she didn't want her family to have me, but I think she fell out of favor with them because she was married and had a child with an older man. Six months later, he married Francis (Fran).

As I was writing this book, I realized that Big Eddie and Fran were then almost fifty years old, and both did not know how or probably did not care how to provide the attention that an one year old needed, because Big Eddie and Fran were really the age of grandparents. Big Eddie had never raised any young children before, and that was Fran's first encounter in a long time with a young child; therefore, while they lived their lives, I had to keep up and just had to deal with it. Big Eddie married Fran primarily to keep his family together avoiding the State of New York Courts from giving me to Marilyn's family. Fran adopted me, and instantly I had a new family that included a twenty-five year old stepbrother named Ricky, five aunts, one uncle, and many cousins in their mid-twenties. My cousins didn't like me because I got into a lot of arguments with them mainly because I was Fran's favorite and both she and Big Eddie would take my side all the time. But as I reflect back on those moments, I understand now that Big Eddie and Fran were forcing her adult nieces and nephews to accept and play crucial roles in my young life when those adults were busy trying to control their own lives filled with sex, drugs, and alcohol.

According to Big Eddie, when he met Fran, she was tall, light-skinned, and a stunning knockout. She was born in South Carolina, she was the youngest of seven children, and she lived in Brooklyn with her sister when Big Eddie met her.

From what I can remember, Fran and Big Eddie had issues with Ricky, who was a tall, strongly built (physically intimidating) alcoholic and a drug addict (he primarily smoked crack). To me, he was a cool brother who did not teach me about life, and I do not have many memories of him, but I remember Big Eddie and Fran had a huge argument after Ricky slapped Fran because she didn't provide him any money, and Big Eddie wanted him out of the apartment. I also remember one night I woke up to the smell of gasoline because Ricky stole a motorcycle and brought it into the house, and Big Eddie made him take it out because the smell of gasoline was killing us. The most dangerous part of that was all three of them were smokers. Last I heard (in August 2001) Ricky was on death row in North Carolina for killing his wife (who was a preacher) by snapping her neck because she wouldn't give him any money during his two-day crack high. After he killed her, he cleaned the dishes and swept and mopped the floors (around her body), and it wasn't until her son came home and saw his mother on the floor unresponsive that the police were called. I think I was sometimes loved by Fran's family, but I never felt loved because I was always introduced as "Fran's step kid," and Big Eddie hated that term. I understood that we were not blood, but he believed a child shouldn't be introduced as a "step-child." Nonetheless, living in a household with family members who were adults, I witnessed many crazy and uncomfortable moments. However, out of all the people I encountered, Big Eddie was the most influential person in my life.

To understand who I am, you have to understand who Big Eddie was. Big Eddie was born in 1927, in Tennessee, and he died in 2001, in Brooklyn. He was the youngest child from Samuel Sr. and Eve, and his siblings included his brothers Samuel Jr. and Willie and his sisters Georgia and Annie. I do not know much about his childhood and young adulthood (as a matter of fact, I never met anyone related to him), but I remember when I was a young boy, he told me that when he was fourteen years old he parted from his family because he witnessed a terrifying event. He stated he left because one night when he finished using the outhouse, he witnessed a black man lynched by a white mob. Big Eddie said, "I heard people screaming, yelling, and holding sticks with fire blazing. I witnessed a crowd of around twenty white men with children, and two of the men placed a rope around a black man's neck and pulled on the rope, lifted him up while he was hanging from a tree branch. He wiggled, and one of the white men shot him in his private area, and the black man suddenly stopped moving, and two days later, without saying goodbye to my father and my mother, I escaped to New York City." That story stayed with me and it sparked my interest learning about lynching, and I used it to write my master's thesis.

13

My father was a young very handsome man, who somehow, when he arrived in New York, he met and lived with an older beautiful black woman, had children, then moved on to other women and had more children. You would say he was a rolling stone. In the early 1950s, while hanging out in a club, he met a young sailor (who was a few years older) named Ken who was honorably discharged from the navy. Ken was a medium height, very light-skinned skinny man, and he bought a three-story, four-bedroom brownstone in the Crown Heights section of Brooklyn. Big Eddie lived with him while he taught my father about cooking and meeting women, and decades later Ken became my godfather. However, Big Eddie also hung around drug dealers, number runners, and street hustlers, so he grew up understanding survival and violence as his way to avoid failing. In the early 1970s, Big Eddie was a janitor for Kings County Hospital, and he kept a very clean home (as I do too). I never really appreciated and accepted him until I was thirteen years old because I was ashamed of him because I did not understand who he really was. He never forgot how to get home after drinking all night, and from the time I could remember he always was an alcoholic but never a drunk. I never saw him fall down steps, pass out, or not know where he was, but his drinking added with his old age embarrassed me. I remember one embarrassing moment when I was in the sixth grade and we were at a parent-teacher conference. For some reason my principal got loud with him, and so he went into the restroom, drank some of his pint of Bacardi dark (from his back pocket), returned, and rained a verbal assault at my principal (classic Big Eddie).

I am the youngest of his twelve children (I never met any of them), and I was joked on a lot because my friends laughed about his age compared to their much younger fathers. However, when I became older, many of their fathers had major personal issues that I wouldn't trade Big Eddie's alcoholism and his old age for. He became a friend to me, but he also made me understand the thin line between friendship and parenting, and when I crossed that line, he reminded me of the consequences. One time when I was thirteen years old, we were kidding with each other and I called him an old man, and before I could walk away, he punched the crap out of me right in my stomach, then he laughed while I tried to catch my breath. He was a medium-built, brown-skinned, and gray-haired man who wore outdated black framed glasses, but he was strong as an ox. Hearing him say "I brought you in this world, and I'll take you out!" added to his verbal intimidation especially since he started saying that around the time when Marvin Gaye was killed by his own father. I used to hang out with my father on the corners, at gambling spots (called "number spots"), and around women. Several times, he told those women, "Stick your hand in my pocket," and when they did, they rubbed on his penis. He also made statements like "Hey good-looking," "Watch what I can do with my tongue," and other crazy sayings. He always told me, "You better not tell your mother about what you saw, or I will beat your ass."

When I became a teenager, he became larger than life to me, and he knew that I would have to come into my own, and so he educated me with street knowledge no matter the subject or environment; he was a street-smart genius. He taught me to depend on myself, and if I had to do something, then do it myself because I would still be fine. He constantly told me, "You were born by yourself, and you will die by yourself," and "One monkey won't stop your show!" He explained situations to me that I would (and did) face and told me how to get out of them by either fighting or talking, but it would take me to use my brain to survive those situations. That was a major difference between my father and my friends' fathers since Big Eddie always made sure I understood what he was educating me on. Because he was older, he had been through all the situations a young black boy and black man faced. Other fathers who were much younger probably could only tell their sons what to do and what not to do. When I did fall or did something that I should not have done, he never showed that he was mad at me for not seeing things I should have seen, but he quietly looked at me with a "you've learned the hard way today, so next time you will see situations clearly."

Besides the daily sex talk, and to never hit a woman, he taught me key important street skills such as just because you shake hands and drink with people, it doesn't mean they are your friends. Never walk the streets with your head down looking at the ground because that informs people that you are a pushover, and the wolves in the streets will treat you like sheep, and you will be a victim. People who drag their feet are lazy, so stay away from them because if they are too lazy to pick up their feet, they are lazy at other things in their lives (this I should have really paid attention to). If I was to ever smoke, never smoke anything you didn't see made in front of you because you never know what someone puts in their cigarettes or joint. There were true examples of this. I remember when a guy I knew who was both physically and verbally intimidating all of a sudden turned into a frightened dude after he smoked marijuana laced with either cocaine or crack because two guys he knew gave it to him while they were smoking it. The guys couldn't say no to him because they would have had to explain what they were smoking, so instead of being known as guys who smoked cocaine or crack, they let their "friend" smoke it. Big Eddie also explained to me why he did not know any of his other children. He told me that he didn't get along with their mothers, and instead of staying with them and caring for the children, he decided to leave, so he and their mothers wouldn't have to kill each other. Since he didn't fully explain all the details, I said to myself, "How could that be? How could you not see your children every day or even talk to them or make some kind of contact?" I look back at that conversation a lot since I was in that situation with my oldest daughter and now understand how relationships can become complicated.

My father's wisdom was and still is priceless. He informed me of my future mistakes, and many times he stopped me before I made them. He was terrific at reading people, and only after he had enough of someone's bull, he let them know that they were liars and/or phonies. Of the guys I hung out with (even his adult friends), he informed me who shared my best interest, who would leave me in a fight, (he was always dead-on), and who would get me in trouble. He taught me the difference between how to live with a woman and how to love the right woman from his experiences and by letting me hear and explaining to me the music he listened to. He taught me the qualities of a good girlfriend, the kind of woman who I needed to love, to spend the rest of my life with, and he even told me when I was in high school that I would marry Chris. He stated that I can love a woman, but I should never need a woman. That meant that I should never depend on a woman (or anyone). He told me to never live with a woman who refuses to work or cannot offer anything financially to the relationship because I can do bad by myself, and if I fall financially, she can keep us afloat. He used to say that a jealous man cannot work, and to never have intercourse with any of my closest friends' girlfriends because girls come and go, but the drama you will have will last forever. Big Eddie told me almost a thousand times, "Always remember this. You can't have sex with everybody, and you don't want to either." Also, he told me that for both a man and a woman that "If you don't take care of home, then someone else will." Meaning there shouldn't be any reason for your lover to leave you if you are doing what you need to do at home financially, emotionally, and physically. Adding to his legend, he was a master ghetto chef. He fed you before he drank with you because he always stated, "You can't drink on an empty stomach!" He embraced and educated my real friends, and as a matter a fact, they treated him as their father. His knowledge kept us alive and out of prison.

We lived in the Flatbush section of Brooklyn. My building was across the street from Prospect Park, and the neighborhood included many low-income families. I stayed in the house a lot and I also got into trouble. One time, I was on a ladder stealing cookies out of the cookie jar. Then Big Eddie and Fran saw me after around seven cookies, I turned around, saw him, and almost fell off the ladder. I received many beatings; therefore, I somehow created hiding places in my room, but that didn't work because Big Eddie found me and beat me without any pants on because he always said, "I'm not tearing up any clothes I bought." I watched a lot of television especially shows such as *The Twilight Zone*, *I Love Lucy*, *The Honeymooners*, *Sanford and Son*, *All in the Family*, and *The Jeffersons*, so I grew up watching mysteries, love and also racist and hateful language. I also watched movies that were definitely not for me to see such as *The Texas Chainsaw Massacre*, *Friday the 13th*, *48 Hours*, *Penitentiary*, *Uptown Saturday Night*, and *Night Shift* (about two white men running a brothel with street hookers out of a morgue).

I watched baseball games by myself since I was the only one in my house who liked baseball. The first game I watched was when the 1985 New York Mets played the Chicago Cubs at Wrigley Field. The Mets stole my soul because Darryl Strawberry and Dwight "Doc" Gooden pulled me in, and I immediately started playing baseball with my toy men. That was (and still is) my favorite sport, and in fact, one time I received a free ticket to a game (a touch the sky seat) from the back of a Frosted Flakes cereal box from a kid I knew. I got on two different trains that connected from Brooklyn to Queens, and I entered Shea Stadium alone with only $1.25 to get back home (the ticket also provided a free drink and a scoop of ice cream inside a small toy helmet), and I was only ten years old!

I loved hanging out with my father, but he was rough on me. I remember the first time I was in a fight, when I was eight years old and hanging out with my father, and one of his friends' eight year old son was there playing with me. Out of nowhere, he poured ketchup on top of my head and laughed, and Big Eddie told me to beat his ass or Big Eddie would beat my ass. We were out there swinging at each other, and I beat the crap out of him and was rewarded with love from my father and his friends, who were drinking, smoking, and cheering us on like we were the entertainment of the night. Because of that moment, I became a nervous kid when I was around other kids including my friends and classmates. I always kept my guard up because I didn't know what they would say or do to me that then I would have to fight about.

We were poor since we lived off social security checks we received because of my mother's death and also Fran's disability insurance check, each between five hundred and seven hundred dollars, which were cashed on the first and fifteenth of each month. I remember when I was around nine years old, my parents used to take me with them to the check cashing place, and thugs would be around the place looking to follow people who cashed their checks to rob them. That forced me to grow up fast because I became sort of a bodyguard or protector, and that has stuck with me to this day. Looking back on those moments, I thought I was with them because no one was home to watch me. Big Eddie and Fran sometimes went at different times, so one of them could have watched me. There were times when I was "loaned out" to go with their women friends when they cashed their checks later the same day. It was crazy because in the dangerous rough neighborhood we lived in, how was I going to be able to stop an adult or wild teenager from committing robbery? In fact, I continued to go with Big Eddie until I turned twenty years old. I thank *God* and *Jesus Christ* to this day that nothing ever happened during those times.

With paying for food, rent, and other important items such as alcohol, we were broke within days, and my father would hang out all night with his friends just to ask for and receive some money from them (when I was a teenager, I did this to pay for food and bus fare). Many times, he woke me up as soon as he came home between 1:00 a.m. and 3:00 a.m. (even on school nights) and made me eat the cut-up franks and pork and beans he cooked. When he was out all day, I would be in the house trying to eat anything I found. I ate boiled eggs and cans of Spam. I remember eating cans of sardines, Vienna sausages, oodles of noodles, grilled cheese sandwiches made from the brown boxes of government cheese, powdered milk, and powdered eggs, and many times we made cake mix and Jiffy muffin mix as pancakes for dinner. When we ran out of milk, I ate cereal with water, and once

I used strawberry soda. One time, Ricky had a "friend" who owned an outside icee cart, and he gave a gallon of lemon icee to Ricky (I think he stole it), and we ate that big giant bucket for the whole week for snacks and one night for dinner. Many nights, I just ate candy for dinner (this is why I love eating candy to this day). Big Eddie and Fran constantly asked their friends and neighbors for money (I later realized that was the norm for many families who at least lived in Flatbush). I went to one of our neighbors who lived directly under us on the second floor, and because she barely opened the door (like she was scared as if she did not know me), I gave her a note, and she just stuck her hand out with cash folded up. We were so broke that many times we used newspaper for toilet tissue, and a roll of toilet tissue cost less than a dollar!

We also had a lot of roaches and mice in our house. I vividly remember not eating cereal for a few days after I opened up a box of cereal and roaches ran out of it. I don't remember ever having a birthday cake or a birthday party. It is because of those times that I am not fond of birthday parties, singing "Happy Birthday" at parties, or watching people singing it on television or in movies. I don't even celebrate my birthday or care if someone doesn't call me on my birthday or any holiday. Also, I never had costumes for Halloween, and every year we had the same Christmas table tree and received gifts such as socks, underwear, and one toy. I went to elementary school and I entered straight into the first grade. I was a smart child, but I had a speech impediment since I couldn't enunciate many words (I still cannot), and that made me feel insecure about myself to read out loud because I felt my classmates were going to laugh at me. I did not have the nicest clothes or sneakers, and I did not even have many clothes, but they were clean, and I looked clean.

During both second and third grades, I was pulled out of class once a week and sat with a speech therapist right outside my class door, and I felt embarrassed. The majority of children who attended my school came from different neighborhoods, and all the kids on my block had to walk at least four blocks into a different part of Flatbush to get there. We all knew that the kids who lived on those blocks didn't like other kids walking on their blocks, and sometimes we saw teenagers from those blocks rob fourth and fifth graders, so parents from our block took turns walking us to school and picking us up when we were in the first grade, then they stopped, and we started walking by ourselves in groups. I was ashamed of my father when he picked us up because he always had a friend or two with him, and he always had an empty wet cup since he just finished drinking a cup of beer or wine, primarily Thunderbird.

Big Eddie and Fran weren't very educated. He had never entered high school, and she had only graduated high school. One of my father's true friends, our nonblood "Uncle Floyd," helped me with learning math, reading, and homework. Isn't that something, and he had barely passed the ninth grade (the blind leading the blind). Big Eddie used to threaten me with "If you don't do that homework in an hour, I'm kicking your ass." I had many dried tearstains on my notebook pages, and I knew that saving for college tuition instead of buying food was not an option. I heard and once wondered about college; however, I never dreamed about going especially once I was in the streets. College was for the nerds, and you couldn't even appear to be smart unless you were already in honor classes, and the streets didn't give the smart ones a free pass. Being smart meant you were trying to show off, or you were a sellout. Also, there weren't any financial aid commercials on television (that I saw), which would have explained that you didn't need a million dollars to go to college. The only commercials I saw were the ones that had white people stating, "We have to save for little Johnny's college fund" or a black voice stating, "A mind is a terrible thing to waste." True, but if we don't have money or barely have enough money to buy food and pay bills, how in the hell are my parents supposed to save money for my college tuition? How are we going to go to college with financial aid that creates debt (by the way, a good debt)? College wasn't on my mind especially because I hated when I had to read out loud in class; of course I could read, but I didn't want kids laughing at my speech, and I sure didn't want them to know how smart I really was. What's a kid from a dog-eat-dog environment to do?

We were already asking people to loan us money for food, and when we bought food, it was straight no-frills, those all-white boxes of cereal with no ingredients just the title in bold black letters: "CEREAL." I used to stand in a long line with my father in front of a church once a week to receive free government food items while my friends and classmates saw me. We could not save for college especially with food stamps, and I'm not talking about the food stamp system we have today with the debit card (that would have been great), I'm talking purple, red, and brown money without any dead presidents' faces. I used to sneak the money to the cashier when no one was looking or toss it hard behind the bulletproof glass of the Chinese restaurant hoping they wouldn't call me out about it.

Big Eddie and Fran loved each other, but they definitely had extramarital affairs with their friends or coworkers. They had heated verbal assaults that I heard, and they would make up sexually, and we heard that too. But in the 1980s, Fran was diagnosed with breast cancer, and it spread all over her body. She was 95 percent bedridden, and she wore wigs since she lost at least 95 percent of her hair, but she never stopped drinking and smoking. We took turns bathing and also cleaning her after bowel movements because even though she had a toilet near her bed, sometimes she couldn't get up fast enough to use it. I remember when I was around eight years old and having to bathe and put lotion on her front and back side (even on her breast) because it helped her with her pain. Can you imagine how I felt and how embarrassed she must have felt? Fran was very skinny and fragile, but she did not take any crap and wouldn't back down to anyone. I remember one time a teenage girl (around eighteen years old) who lived on the second floor of our building was messing with me. Fran found the strength, and we went to the girl's apartment because Fran wanted to talk with her mother (who was not there), and the girl (who knew us) screamed at Fran and pulled her wig off, and the kids there laughed. An embarrassing moment for us and hopefully for the girl. Because she was sick and physically unable to provide for Big Eddie's sexual needs, they agreed that he could step out of their marriage as long as it was never brought up, and I heard this agreement. That was easy for him since he didn't work anymore and just played in the streets on the hunt. There were times when he left us for two to three days. He told us that he worked for the mob, but really what he was doing was staying at his girlfriend's apartment. He was very smart and slick about it, making two days of food so we would have enough to eat.

I hated those times, and I really hated him when I found out what he was really doing. One day while I was playing baseball in my living room by myself, I hit the paper made baseball up high, and it landed on top of a speaker hanging in the left-hand corner of the living room. I stepped on a chair and reached for the ball, and I found a picture of him and his girlfriend dressed up sitting at a dinner table at a restaurant French kissing (I never seen anything like that before). Who would actually agree to take a picture for someone like that? Those times I did not care for him too much since although he took care of my mother, I didn't understand his sexual needs. Of course, Fran's side of her family didn't like it, but they all understood Big Eddie and Fran's agreement. I remember as a child hearing many arguments between one of her nephews (who lived with us) and Big Eddie regarding how he broke Fran's hip while having sex, and he always screamed back at her nephew in a powerful but ashamed loud voice, "Fran wanted it too, damn it! She asked me to make her feel wanted like a beautiful woman again."

During the 1980s, as far as I can remember, there were always a lot of people, cigarettes, drugs, and alcohol in my household. For example, I took my first drink of alcohol from a shot glass on top of the living room table when I was six years old. I remember when I was around eight years old going to the liquor store on the corner to pay Big Eddie and Fran's monthly liquor bill and returning the next day to pick up a gallon of Bacardi dark. I remember when I was seven years old and my father, Uncle Floyd, and my cousins (Fran's nephews) Greg and Kevin were playing poker. Kevin was very short, born with one kidney, and a crack addict. Many times, he used to smoke it in his cigarettes. As I was growing up, nothing was more horrible and disgusting than being a crackhead, and they were disrespected all the time. Especially drug dealers would either rob them, beat them up, or even get them to do sexual acts. When my father was winning, I would come up to him and he would "pay me" for being his good luck. I guess Kevin got tired of him taking all his money, and he told me, "Get your ass out of here." My father laughed, and I said to Kevin, "You're just mad because you're losing all your money." As I walked away, he threw a full closed pint of vodka and hit me in my back between my shoulder blades, and it didn't hurt but I was shocked. I turned around and saw Kevin sitting there looking at me mad and slightly smiling like a devil while everyone screamed profanity down upon his face. Later around 2:00 a.m. I got up from sleeping to use the only bathroom we had, and I saw him standing in front of the mirror smoking crack while the door was cracked open (my first time and unfortunately, not my last time ever seeing that). At least three of my cousins and Ricky were crack addicts, and so were some of their friends and a few of my father's friends.

Until I got married, I witnessed people doing hard drugs in front of me as if it were normal. Cut straws (for cocaine), empty cocaine bags on the sink, used needles found on top of the bathroom medicine cabinet (open the cabinet and they fall into the sink), burned crack pipes, burned chicken bones, burned open ended pens, burned match stems, and the burned rubber smell were all normal in my childhood. As a child, I watched perfectly normal adults enter my bathroom only to come out crazy and/or deranged zombies who either were strong enough to take on the world or scared running across the room screaming because they were being chased by large pink elephants holding steak knives. Moreover, what goes perfectly with drugs and alcohol? Sex.

We had a lot of cousins, uncles, friends, and friends of friends stay with us, and because of the environment, I sometimes gave up our room for others to have sexual relations. Those times were really wild especially when finding used condoms under my bed or on the floor between my bed and my dresser. One time we rented WrestleMania on cable television, and there were ten of my friends and ten of my father's friends (a full house). Man, I loved watching and playing wrestling as a kid because most of my friends did (up until the middle of seventh grade). We wanted to wrestle on the bed mattress in my room before the main event started (Hulk Hogan vs. The Ultimate Warrior). We walked into my room, and

Greg was cracked out his mind laying butt naked having sex with one of my friend's crack addict sister with crack pipes on the nearby end table and their eyes looked like four tomatoes.

My bright spots when I was a child and teenager were my Uncle Clarence, Uncle Wayne, and my grandmother Addie. She was married to my grandfather Clarence Sr., but she wasn't Marilyn's mother. Clarence and Wayne never had children; therefore, I was his only nephew. Big Eddie knew my uncles since they were little boys because he hung out with Clarence Sr. (Big Eddie gave my uncles their first drink of alcohol). I didn't get to meet my Uncle Clarence until I was twelve years old. He lived only twenty minutes away in another rough part of Flatbush, and his building was a haven for drug deals and a lot of crime. As a matter of fact, the first time I visited my uncle, it was in the middle of the day, and there were several drug deals in the lobby. I also saw several apartment doors (including my uncle's) that had gray masking tape blocking holes where locks used to be because they were knocked out after attempts of breaking into those apartments. Big Eddie told me about him and showed me a picture, and in the picture, he was a tall, mid-twenties, dark-skinned black man with a baseball bat and a US Postal Service softball shirt on. He worked for the post office in Manhattan, New York, at the time (he died in the bathroom at that location on his fortieth anniversary), and I was excited to meet him not

31

because he was someone I hoped would be different from the adults I lived with (he was), but because he played softball, and that meant he loved baseball. He embraced all sports, and he was the only person I knew who did that.

When we met, he immediately understood that I loved sports especially baseball, and within a month, he took me to the old Yankee Stadium to see the Yankees host the Cleveland Indians, and from that moment, I fell in love with the Yankees. He took me to see a few of his softball games, a few of his basketball games (he played or was a referee), and some summers he took me to Upstate New York on weekends because his coworkers had their annual weekend cookout with their families and friends. He also took me to Virginia, to spend a week, Thanksgiving, or Christmas with my grandmother and their side of their family. My Uncle Clarence was a good man and loved by his friends and family. He smiled and laughed a lot, he hung around good people, and he kept his share of good-looking girlfriends. He was born and raised in Brooklyn, and he became an outstanding basketball star in high school, and because of his smooth and dangerous jump shot, he was scouted by several colleges. My Uncles Clarence and Wayne were total opposites. Clarence was the star, and Wayne was the oldest and the one constantly in trouble. When they were teenagers, my Uncle Wayne was involved with a few bad guys, he got hurt, and he became paralyzed from the waist down. Instead of my Uncle Clarence taking a scholarship and leaving for college, he enrolled in a community college and helped his brother and mother, who both eventually moved to Virginia where she had grown up with her large family.

My uncle and I played baseball games on my Sega Genesis until 2:00 a.m. I was the Toronto Blue Jays (I loved them since 1990) and he was the Yankees. I used to think to myself that I would love to visit the Sky Dome (currently the Rogers Centre) because I thought one day he would take me; however, it was in Canada, and there weren't any miracles I foresaw to get me there. A few years later, he took me to a couple of parties, and when I was fifteen years old, I was his best man and only witness at his wedding, but unfortunately the marriage only lasted a few months. I also helped him move from his drug and crime infested building into the top floor of his former manager's two-story home in Jamaica, Queens, NY. Ironically, it was around the corner from Chris's great-grandmother's home, and Chris and I never knew it. I used to visit him a few times, and those times could have been moments when Chris and I just missed each other.

I believed almost every family who lived in the Flatbush area had some kind of problem whether it was not having money or not enough of it, being on welfare, having broken families, or/and having criminals in their families. That was the early and mid-1980s, and a time when hip-hop was coming into its own expressing lyrics of sex, drugs, crime, and jail, and young children and teenagers who were exposed to it soaked it up. Drugs were slowly moving from needles and snorting cocaine to smoking crack, so people had to be careful walking the streets because young and hungry stick-up kids and crazy drug addicts were among the criminals robbing and hurting people for gold, money, and even clothing. I remember when people were being robbed, shot, and several killed almost every day for their 8 Ball leather jackets. I remember one of my parents' friends who used to come by our apartment suddenly stopped coming because her grandchild was killed when her apartment was shot up with bullets.

One evening in 1986, I was playing with two kids I knew my age in one of the buildings one of their grandparents lived in. He stated he had to go upstairs to his grandmother's apartment to grab something to drink and so we went with him. It was located on the top floor of the four-story building, as soon as we walked in, to the left was his Uncle Andre's room. Andre was watching television with some of his teenage friends, and we went in the back of the apartment to the kitchen and my friend introduced me to his grandparents named Big Mommy and Big James. Big Mommy asked me if I wanted something to eat, I said yes, and I stayed. Because in my apartment we barely had food, it was normal for me to go to my friends' homes and stay until they ate dinner. I believe their parents knew, but I don't think it bothered them. That moment changed my life because before that moment, I played only in my building but all that changed when I met Andre.

I didn't start hanging out with Andre until close to Halloween since the NFL football season was starting. One day I came outside and he and other kids I knew from my block were playing football. Andre yelled at me, "Hey, you! Wanta play? Can you catch?" That moment changed my life! I started playing and from that day, I started watching football, became a fan of the New York Giants, and soon, I was known as one of his fastest and trusted wide receivers (a huge deal). Andre was a tall and heavy teenager who was literally larger than life to mostly all of the children and teenagers. He was all about the hip hop culture. He had all the dope gear, a thick gold chain, two weeks of sneakers which he cleaned with a toothbrush and a small clear plastic cup filled with detergent and hot water. He ate ice cream out of a cup even in the winter time, and he played R&B songs from Keith Sweat, and he had hip hop posters all over his room which included LL Cool J, Salt N Pepper, Slick Rick, Big Daddy Kane, and Kool G Rap just to name a few. He always shared his knowledge about the streets and how to talk to girls.

Andre had a lot of nephews and cousins who were becoming or already were wolves and monsters, and a few of them were around my age or a year older. During those times, I learned the streets mostly from Andre, but while I hung around his nephews and cousins, I grew more knowledgeable about the streets than school. Now as an adult, I understand that each one of them crossed a line while surviving in several dog-eat-dog environments. Over time, I began to be known as Andre's right-hand man, and I became an unofficial family member as his family welcomed me and I will always appreciate each one of them for that. However, my first personal and frightening moment of understanding that we lived in a crime infested environment was when I was probably ten years old, and Big Eddie was robbed on the first floor of our building in the afternoon. I was playing outside, and I was told that my father was robbed and stripped naked while checking the mail (this is the primary reason I always look around). As a child, I thought crime will always be part of my life, and I realized that crimes don't only happen at night. Later that day, the detectives came to my home, and took me and my father to the precinct so he could look at mugshots. Every thick book of mugshots he finished looking at, I picked up and looked at, and I recognized a few of the people in those books.

After that, Big Eddie spent a lot of time with Eleanor, who was his longtime girlfriend. Eleanor and her family treated me like family during the time I was becoming a young teenager, and I followed them around like a puppy. I believe Eleanor had seven kids, and all were at least twenty-five years old when I met them. Chad was a tall, dark, medium-built guy, and a real smooth talker who could con you to give him your last pennies, to jump off the roof with the "special" sneakers he sold you, or just make a woman spend money on him. He was a major influence in my life since I took some of his persona and sometimes his clothes. Doug was my man. He was a tall, built guy and a straight knockout artist (physically and verbally intimidating), and he was a funny guy who told jokes, but he wouldn't hesitate to put your lights out. He was the type of guy you have to shoot just to slow him down, and man, I wanted to be like him; he was the reason I worked out and lifted weights. Chad and Doug took me on as their little brother, and I will always thank them for that. They were two of the few men who provided me knowledge of the streets and about women. Man, when I was a teenager, I went to adult parties with them, and I always had a great time. As an adult looking back on those times, I understand that the home environment and family relationships I lived in were based solely on an adult world.

Big Eddie also hung out with cool women friends, and one of them was named Iris. She was a full-figured tall black woman with a big heart, and she was married for three years to Rockmond (a quiet but hardcore guy straight off the boat from Jamaica who one could barely understand), and they had a daughter around the age of five years old. Iris also had two kids prior to her marriage who were young adults, but she was cheating on Rockmond with Jasper (a cool Jamaican guy who always gave me money). I guess she and Rockmond had an agreement that she could step outside their marriage because they only married so he could receive a green card, she just could never let him know about it. Iris and Jasper would occasionally meet at my house and sometimes have sex in my room (perhaps that was the reason he always gave me money).

In December 1990, my parents had a small party with some of both of their friends, and on that particular night, Big Eddie was supposed to spend the night at Eleanor's house (she lived in Flatbush almost twenty minutes away). However, he drank a lot and decided to stay home, and Iris was drunk, so she spent the night with her youngest daughter. Although Fran was bedridden with cancer, she smoked cigarettes and drank alcohol. Around 3:00 a.m., Big Eddie woke up and used the bathroom (maybe 200 feet from their bedroom), and at that time, Fran was in the dark smoking in the bed. She knocked her glass of liquor on the floor between her bed and her end table, she tried to wipe it up, her cigarette dropped and quickly started a fire. She screamed, but we didn't hear her, and luckily Big Eddie happened to walk out of the bathroom and saw the flames. He quickly ran into the bedroom and carried her out into the building hallway. She had minor burns on her legs, then he ran back inside the apartment, past the flames, and straight to the back rooms and woke up Iris, her daughter, and me as the fire quickly spread throughout the apartment. Then we started knocking on our neighbors' doors making them aware of the fire. Thanks to *God* and *Jesus Christ*, we survived. By the time the fire department arrived, and the smoke settled, we lost 90 percent of everything, and we were officially homeless. The clothes that were not burned smelled heavier of smoke but I had to wear them; however, a few parents from my block gave me some clothes, but their kids laughed at me for wearing their "hand-me-downs" (it is no wonder why I barely trust anyone). We did not have one place for all of us to live, so Big Eddie and Fran went to live with my aunt (Fran's sister) in one of the worst, toughest, and realest housing developments (projects) located in Brownsville, Brooklyn. So that I could continue the seventh grade in the same school, for a week, I ate and slept at several of Big Eddie's friends' apartments then I stayed with Iris and Rockmond on an unfamiliar block with unfamiliar guys three blocks from my old apartment.

A few days later, my father talked to me while at his friend Big Tony's apartment, and he stated, "We have two choices. Either we could wait for our apartment to be fixed and ready to move back in within six months, or we can move into the projects within a few weeks. They (New York State

Housing Authority) said it's between five projects in Brooklyn, but we will not know until two weeks before we move in. The choice is up to you." I knew whatever projects we were to live in would be extremely rough and real, but I also knew that we couldn't live away from each other for six months especially with Fran's condition. In addition, I was really tired of people laughing at me for wearing the clothes I desperately needed. I said, "Let's move to the projects!" That decision would definitely change me forever. Big Eddie's courage and patience throughout that whole situation made me love and embrace him while our relationship started to grow.

I went to live with Iris and Rockmond in early January. They lived on the third floor of a rental townhouse, and looking back, I think it probably was Section 8 housing because Iris did not work, she used food stamps a lot, and Rockmond had a job but wasn't paid a lot. I was extremely grateful for having a roof over my head and food in my stomach; however, their apartment was extremely small. I slept on the twin bed that was straight across the kitchen, and some nights they left the light on, so I saw the mice chasing each other heading behind the stove. Sometimes the heat wouldn't work, and sometimes we had only cold water, and because the apartment did not have a shower, it would be weeks until I took my next shower so we all just washed up instead. Sometimes we didn't have toothpaste, and for a few days, I didn't have a toothbrush. For those times, I brushed my teeth with salt and water on my finger. One day in March 1991, I came home from school around 3:30 p.m. and saw police caution tape across Iris's door (I didn't have a key). I left and went to Big Tony's, and I called Big Eddie. He informed me that Rockmond had beat Iris almost to death using a long heavy-duty workout bending rod (probably because she bragged about her sexual relationship with Jasper). Fortunately, we were days away from moving into the projects. Rockmond was arrested, and Iris was in the hospital for two weeks.

Little Eddie Becomes Eddie
(1991–1992)—Eddie's POV

In April 1991, we moved into a housing project in the Canarsie section of Brooklyn, which is sandwiched between Brownsville and East New York; all three neighborhoods are filled with projects, dangerous people, and crime. Fran wasn't in any physical shape to continue to be cared for by us because she needed around the clock medical care; therefore, we placed her in a nice nursing home in Flatbush only an hour away from us. We spent time with her twice a week, and we even brought her home and gave her a birthday party with her sister and most of her nieces and nephews there. Her condition became worse because she could only eat through a tube through the side of her stomach, and she repeatedly pulled the tube out, and that put her in a life-threatening situation because her temperature and high blood pressure both rose.

I lived on the third floor with Big Eddie, but Pete (who was one of Eleanor's daughter's children's father and great friend of Big Eddie), Kevin, and Chad lived with us for a few years. Again, thanks to *God* and *Jesus Christ*, I arrived at the right time since my peers were just coming into their own with playing basketball, football, and wilding out. As a young man entering into a new area especially the projects, it can become challenging, but I met the right kid at the right time. During the first week, I sat at the basketball court, and I met a teenager named Tyrone (Ty). Ty was a few months older than I was, in the eighth grade, but he was around my height and body type. He introduced himself, and days later, we just started to hang. He was looking for a guy like me, and I was looking for a guy like him. Everyone knew Ty, and he knew everyone and everyone's business.

Ty lived with his mother who was in a long-time relationship with her boyfriend, and Ty had three brothers. Big Eddie loved Ty, and he loved Big Eddie. We started running in the streets together. He introduced me to almost everyone in the projects, and everyone showed me love because of Ty. Most of the guys we hung out with were all coming into their own manhood. Those guys were on track for ruthless antics, and I was glad that I was cool with them. He introduced me to guys who robbed, guys who were shot and survived, and guys who were savages and monsters. Within a few weeks, I knew almost everyone in the projects. I had never been the kind of person who wanted to sell drugs because it wasn't my thing, and looking back, it was for three reasons. The first was that I never knew any drug dealers who "had it all" like driving the newest or flashy cars. The drug dealers I knew had shootouts almost every night, and they made money but not enough to get off the corner. The second reason was because of Big Eddie. He wasn't that kind of man; therefore, he never exposed or encouraged me into that world because it wasn't his thing because getting women was mostly his thing. Finally, because I grew up as a R&B fan, I didn't embrace hip hop until Big Daddy Kane's "Ain't No Half-Steppin'." Therefore, when I was a child, I wasn't embedded with the rhymes rappers told of crime and looking up to the rich drug dealers. Although it was in my neighborhood, the drama and realization attached to me later than others even though I grew up listening to The O'Jays and Curtis Mayfield.

During my first month in the projects, I met Darrell, and he lived two doors away on my floor. He was a tall black kid who was two years younger than me, and he lived with his aunt, uncle, and his grandmother. At that time, Darrell's grandmother would let him go outside and play (especially basketball), and she called his name out the hallway window, so we used to joke and laugh at him about that stuff. He was a smart teenager, he had video games, and the best thing was that he embraced all sports, especially baseball. Man, at that time, I never had a friend who loved baseball, so we played baseball games and kept our own stats on paper. We listened to rap songs and studied the lyrics, and I vividly remember when we wrote down and studied the lyrics of most of the songs from the Das EFX's Dead Serious tape when it first came out. His grandmother used to cook all the time, so I stayed there hanging with Darrell until I ate dinner with them. I loved his family! During the summer of that year, Ty introduced me to Lewis. He was a medium-height, light-skinned teenager, and a year older than I was. All three of us connected quickly since we ran together. Lewis didn't like staying in one place too long, so he lived place to place and finally lived with his godmother in the projects, and when he got tired of that, his godmother asked Big Eddie if Lewis could stay with us, Big Eddie agreed. Lewis walked with an "I'm not scared" attitude, and he knew anyone he hung with would have his back. I remember one time when I was in the ninth grade, Ty and I met up a few blocks away from Canarsie High School (Lewis was a student who never went to class). Ty saw a guy chasing Lewis trying to beat him up, and Lewis called out, "Ty! Help me, bro!" Ty ran up to the kid and punched him out. Soon, I met one of my best friends named Rich, who lived in the same projects, and in the next year, I reconnected with another best friend named Bull, who I knew years earlier because my uncle dated Bull's mother for ten years.

In my home, again the bathroom was the place of drug use, but all that was normal to us. Big Eddie always had beer and liquor, and family, friends, and associates were always invited. Many times, Kevin would come out of the bathroom after smoking crack and look like a frightened zombie since he paced and sat down, rubbing his knees extremely fast, and then popped up and started running. Pete used to be so high that several times we had to pick the bathroom lock, pick him up out of the tub, pull his pants and underwear back on him, and clean up the sink that had empty heroin bags. Our bathroom continued to smell like burned rubber with burned matches, crack pipes, and burned empty chicken bones. I remember one time sitting down with two of Big Eddie's friends, and while we all were talking, very casually, one started chopping up a bag of dope, created lines, and both of them took turns snorting and talking to me like it wasn't happening.

I was a horrible student during my first year in high school, actually throughout my entire teenage years. I was hanging out with wolves and monsters. No matter if I was in Flatbush or in the projects, I grew up faster than I should have. I had to learn on my own to play the mental game of chess before I ever played the actual game of checkers. As a child, I started to live in survival mode, spending 90 percent of my life on defense. I had to understand life especially in critical moments. I learned that the streets never slept and were always watching. The streets were like prison, if you were a sheep, then the wolves found you. If you were a wolf, then other wolves found you. Even though wolves understood wolves, they may not respect each other which can lead to a dangerous situation in a heartbeat. It was a very thin line that if crossed by mistake or on purpose, it could lead to prison, fights, neighborhood wars, or even death anytime or anywhere. I had to face those moments every day. Just leaving the building, going to school, or going to the corner store could lead to so much more. Once you crossed into that world, you cannot return to the person you once saw. I had PTSD before I turned a teenager.

During my second week of my freshman year, I was cutting classes to meet girls, and that was when I met Chris. From the start, I knew she was different than any other girl I have ever met (still is). She was sitting next to her friend Tiffany while they sat across the lunchroom table from me and a girl, I was trying to get with named Shanice. I noticed Chris, but I didn't pay her any attention because I knew she wasn't one of those fast girls. She looked like probably dated only the pretty boy types since she was dating the varsity football team quarterback (a pretty boy). I was never an ugly guy, but I wasn't a pretty boy either. Two weeks went by, and Chris watched me chase after that girl. During that time, I noticed Chris looking at me a lot, but I didn't think anything of it.

Chrissy
(1978–1988)—Christina's POV

I was born in 1978, in Kings County Hospital in Brooklyn, NY (the same hospital Eddie was born in four months earlier). I was two months premature weighing only three pounds and one ounce. My mother, Lisa, became pregnant with me at sixteen years old by her high school boyfriend, Jean. From my understanding, Jean and my mother's relationship didn't work out. Alfredo, who was also sixteen years old stepped in to be my father and later married my mother three years later.

I was born premature because my mother had a medical condition called pre-eclampsia which caused her to have high blood pressure, and as a result, I stayed in the Neonatal Intensive Care Unit (NICU) in an incubator for two months until my lungs were fully developed. As a toddler, I had Bronchitis and Pneumonia a couple times. When I was three years old, I had to stay in the hospital for a while on antibiotics, and my entire family stayed by my bedside as I recuperated. I knew from that and later other experiences how much my family cared for me; therefore, I knew I could not let them down and had to make them proud when I became a teenager and an adult. In the 1970s, neonatal medicine was not what it is today. Children born prematurely rarely survived, and in many cases had developmental delays. It was nothing short of a miracle and *God's* blessings that I survived and was not born with defects or special needs. I remember my great-grandmother Mama telling me she prayed in my hospital room and asked everyone to pray for me. I remember once when I was six or seven visiting a wedding reception with Mama, and everyone she encountered was astounded that I was healthy without special needs. There were even whispers "Oh it's amazing she's not slow". However, I was underweight and petite during my childhood and adolescence. I was teased as an adolescent because of it. Those times made me shy and caused me to be introverted.

My mother was born in Queens to her teenage parents, Ellen, and Charles. Ellen and Charles both came from upper-middle class families, which was a major accomplishment for people of color in the 1960s. Ellen raised Lisa and her younger brother, Cory, in the Crown Heights section of Brooklyn and Ellen's mother Enid (Mama) was an immigrant from Panama by way of Barbados. Her family immigrated to New York City by way of Ellis Island in 1923, and for three decades, her family owned three brownstone houses in the Bedford Stuyvesant section of Brooklyn on Jefferson Avenue. In the 1950s, Enid's mother, Viola, purchased property in the Westhampton Beach section of Long Island, NY, which was another major accomplishment and very rare for people of color at that time. Decades later it became a sought-after summer vacation spot for the wealthy known as "The Hamptons". My mother's parents divorced when she was around seven years old. My mother had a good childhood. After I was born, she went back to finish high school while Mama took care of me. I stayed with Mama during the week and went home on the weekends. Mama was like Mrs. Claus to me. She was the sweetest person in the world, and she taught me so much about carrying myself with dignity and respect. I believe I am an old soul because of Mama. An old soul is a spiritual person who is wise beyond their years.

My father, Alfredo, was born in Colon, Panama, he, and his father immigrated to Brooklyn when he was five years old. My father was raised by his father, grandmother, aunts, and his stepmother, Paulina. He grew up to be an intelligent and hardworking man. When my father was eighteen years old, he enlisted in the U.S. Air Force. After he finished Basic Military Training and Tech School in 1981, he came back to Brooklyn and married my mother, and we moved to Sacramento, California (near his base), and while there, they had a son named Antonio (Tony). During that year, my father was discharged, and in 1982, we moved back to Brooklyn. When Alfredo stepped in to be my father, that was a blessing from *God*. He has always been my father and always will be.

We moved into a neighborhood in the Crown Heights section of Brooklyn. My great-grandfather owned a multi-unit building in Crown Heights that we lived in until I was in my early twenties. I met my first best friend, Baria. She was two and I was four years old. We immediately become best friends. She had so much charisma and wore these cute little fancy dresses. I wore a little pocketbook everywhere I went, and that explains my love for handbags. Baria was so smart you would have thought she was two going on twenty-one. We did everything together since we lived next door to each other. Our neighborhood in the 1960s through early 1980s was highly regarded. It was a neighborhood in the 1960s and 1970s inhabited by Jewish and working-class and middle-class people of color. So much so, the movie The Wiz was filmed in our neighborhood, and a block over was where Diana Ross's character, Dorothy, lived in the movie. We had block parties and the annual Brooklyn Children's Museum sponsored June Balloon (a festival). However, in the late 1980s, the crack epidemic emerged and changed our neighborhood, and I witnessed mothers become crack addicts and prostitutes while young men became drug dealers or drug addicts willing to rob anyone for money or valuables to buy crack.

Gunshots became the soundtrack in the evenings while we slept. Our once seemingly safe neighborhood became unsafe, and that placed me in a new frightening world and would provide my first life changing experience. I vividly remember the first time I witnessed a crime while my mother was walking with me and pushing Tony in a stroller, and this guy we didn't know walked up to us and started talking with my mother (that was a distraction), and suddenly, he ripped her gold bracelet from her wrist and ran. I also remember a time when I came home from school and saw a man who was a drug addict, wearing a dirty white T-shirt, hiding in the lobby of my building. That was a very scary moment because I did not know what he would do. Those experiences robbed me of my innocence and forced me to find comfort and an escape in my close-knit family members, events, television, and movies that depicted happiness. This is why I love movies without any drama and with happy endings like the ones on the Hallmark Channel.

One of my favorite places from my neighborhood was my great-grandmother Mama's house in Jamaica, Queens. From the age of five to thirteen, I visited her on the weekends. It was our special time together. Mama always called me "Chrissy" and taught me how to sew, crochet, bake, cook, and be a lady. I enjoyed visiting Mama's house because I pretended that I lived in the suburbs much like the children on television shows in the early 1980s and early 1990s such as *Our House*, *The Hogan Family*, *Family Matters*, and *Full House*. I wanted to live somewhere I could call to have a pizza delivered and walk to school with tree lined streets with manicured lawns, and at Mama's house, I was able to live out my fantasy and feel safe especially without hearing gunshots.

That way of life motivated me to want a similar life for my future family. She explained to me that it was OK for me to be shy and quiet, read books, and play make believe at my little desk while writing checks and letters just as she did. Every day I watched my favorite show, Reading Rainbow, and I slept on my own cot next to Mama's bed. She listened to my dreams and told me I could be anything I wanted to be as long as I worked hard, and she encouraged me to be independent like she was. It is because of Mama that I was motivated to succeed and do great things since Mama frequently stated to me, "You want to be independent like me. Don't let anyone or anything head off your dreams. You have a bright future, and *God* will take care of you if you take care of yourself." Before Mama retired, she was a supervisor for the City of New York and then the State of New York. She became a naturalized citizen as an adult and obtained her GED. She meant the world to me. One frightening moment occurred, when I was seven or eight years old, Mama was diagnosed with cancer and she underwent a mastectomy. I remember visiting her at Memorial Sloan Kettering (a hospital that specializes in cancer treatment in Manhattan, NY). I remember Mama being so jovial and brave. She inspired me with her bravery.

My other favorite place from my neighborhood was at my cousin Tina's (also named Christina) condo in Long Island, NY. She was an elementary school teacher who also grew up in Brooklyn and later in Queens. She always took Tony, my younger brother, Brandon, and me for weekends, sometimes weeks during the summers, and a few Easter and Christmas breaks to spend time with her. Tina took us to the library, Taco Bell (something we did not have in Brooklyn at the time), Adventureland (an amusement park in Long Island), the Hamptons to our family home to visit our cousin Johnny (Tina's brother), and go to the beach and main street in East Hampton and IHOP for breakfast. We loved IHOP because there were all sorts of flavored syrups and breakfast meals like pigs in a blanket and pancakes with happy faces made of whipped cream and chocolate chips. Tina would let us drink a small cup of decaf coffee. We always had fun times with Tina. We also enjoyed that she had cable, which meant we had an opportunity to watch Nickelodeon and The Disney Channel. Tina was petite like me, and she taught me that petite women can do anything.

I have been blessed to have three godmothers, and each one of them is special to me since they treated me like I was each one's daughter, and one of my godmothers is Shamean. My mother met Shamean (or Ann as she was referred to back then) and Rolando (my only godfather) in elementary school. My time with

Shamean was very special because I always felt like I was the apple of Shamean's eye even when we did not see each other for years. She taught me to be an independent and educated woman with goals and ambitions. Shamean has a smile and laugh that could light up a room with her magnetizing personality. She taught me that a black woman can be successful and relatable at the same time. My second blessed godmother is Dorne, and when we spent time together, I felt like time never passed. Dorne's family was my family (Shashu, Sweetie, Tiffany, Lover, C.O., Frenchie, and so many others). I loved spending time with Dorne and her family because we always had the best times, they also called me "Chrissy". Dorne had a record for my birthday that said, "Hey Chris, it's your birthday, happy birthday, Chris." I remember Dorne had a joint birthday party for me and her son Daryll at Chuck E. Cheese, she bought me my very first ring, she took me to buy school clothes, and she taught me how to be a strong woman no matter what circumstances cross my path. Paula is my third blessed godmother. She and my mother met as children since they lived in the same building until they became young adults. Paula taught me how to dance, and when I spent time with her, I wanted to drive like her and have an office with Christmas decorations. I'll never forget the time she took me to one of her dance performances when she danced to the song "Street Life" by Randy Crawford. Because of her, I love that song, and I was so proud and in awe that she performed and invited me to attend. I also wanted to crochet my doll a blanket like Paula did for her daughter, and when I was a teenager, I became a cheerleader at Canarsie High School just as Paula did. I never forgot when Paula took me to the circus and the Ice Capades at Madison Square Garden, and she taught me I could be a mother, have hobbies, and have a career.

My godfather Rolando is a huge influence on my life because he taught me about the history of African Americans, our Caribbean history, and important facts about Brooklyn and NYC. He took me and my siblings to several places that were lasting unforgettable moments in our lives such as seeing the Harlem Globetrotters and various unique experiences. An amazing moment occurred when I was three years old. He took me to 42nd street in Manhattan when the famous Black Panther Huey P. Newton's iconic wicker rattan chair was located there for a limited time period, and Rolando and I sat in it. When I was eighteen, Rolando took me to the famous Sylvia's restaurant in Harlem. That same night we went to the Dru Hill concert at the Apollo Theatre (I had the opportunity to get on stage of the iconic Apollo theater). We would drive around NYC and he would give me a mobile history lesson. He always had these little nuggets and gems of knowledge to drop on me. Rolando's exuberant personality and stories are captivating. He always took the time and supported me during memorable moments such as my birthdays, graduations, and the births of my children. He taught me to be a leader and to always question my choices before making any decision.

My Uncle Cory (my mother's brother) is six years older than I am, but he is more like an older brother than uncle to me. He is a rapper (Problemz), and he taught me about hip hop and how to recognize ill lyrics and beats, and as a result, hip hop became one of my favorite genres of music. My Uncle Mike (my father's brother) taught me that education was vital, and college could be attainable, to try new things, and to seek new adventures in life. My grandmothers, Ellen and Paulina were also positive influences in my life. My grandmother Paulina taught me that I could be a successful and an influential lady since she organized many fundraisers and events including cotillion balls that my brothers and I participated in. Because of those experiences, we learned about our culture and that people of color can be distinguished. My grandmother Ellen taught me to continue to persevere no matter what hand life deals you. She also had a great love of music (all genres) and the game show *Jeopardy*. She was a single mother at a young age and a grandmother at thirty-three, and despite the drama and obstacles she endured, she continued on. I was influenced by her to stand up for myself because she had a "you can't push me over!" attitude. I was also inspired to learn how to drive by her.

Because of the many positive influences in my life, I had a very enjoyable childhood. I was blessed and propelled by the many people in my life who inspired and encouraged me. I loved and embraced my parents because I learned my work ethic from my father. He worked overtime for the telephone company to make sure we had the best things in life, and I thought my mother was the prettiest woman on earth. She was a homemaker for most of our childhood. We had a huge apartment, my mother made pancakes on Saturdays, and we spent weekends visiting and spending time with our extended family. We also had Sunday dinners at Mama's house. As a child, I learned my sense of style and obtained my love of music and movies from my mother. My mother always enjoyed having a good time, and made sure our house was clean, we were clean with nice clothes, and taught us that love was the most important thing in a marriage. My mother and I used to go to the West Village to Gray's Papaya for hot dogs and pina coladas. My mother and I also shopped on 8th Street and SoHo. When I was twenty-one, I had my first official drink with my mom, an Amaretto Sour at a restaurant in the South Village, Café Espanol. My family always went to restaurants, and we visited places such as The American Museum of Natural History in Manhattan, local libraries, and parks in Brooklyn. During the summers, we frequently visited The Brooklyn Heights Promenade, Coney Island, The Brooklyn Aquarium, The Bronx Zoo, Six Flags

Great Adventure, and the Poconos. We had a playroom full of toys, and it was a coveted place all the kids who visited us wanted to play in. My mom bought us birthday cakes every year, and we had birthday parties. We also had Halloween costumes every year. For Christmas, we always had an ocean of toys and gifts under the tree.

In 1983, I went to kindergarten at P.S. 289 across the street from our apartment. My teacher was Mrs. Jackson, and she was a nice lady. I was so shy and nervous to go to school since I was attached to my parents for so many years, I cried for most of the day until snack time and play time. After the first few weeks, I quickly realized that I enjoyed school and excelled there. In first grade my parents sent me to Catholic school, and I also excelled there. We had to wear brown and white plaid uniforms with a brown cardigan every day with either white, light yellow, cream, or brown tights. I brought my lunch to school in a lunch box and rode a van with other kids in our neighborhood to and from school. The dress code was really strict; I remember once a girl wore navy tights, and she was reprimanded and then sent home. One Monday morning, my mom didn't have an opportunity to wash my tights, and I only had burgundy cable tights to wear. My mother thought it was close enough to brown, and I wore them to school. That same day our teacher, Ms. Compton, asked us to each sing a song that we loved in front of the class. Most students sang gospel songs. In my house at that time we mostly listened to R&B on 98.7 Kiss FM, so I only knew those songs. I stood on top of the round table that I shared with three other students and sang Tina Turner's hit song at the time "What's Love Got to Do with It." Ms. Compton laughed and then reprimanded me, not for standing on top of the table but for wearing burgundy tights. It was at that moment I learned that I was becoming a fearless and determined young woman. My youngest brother, Brandon, was born in 1984, and I was so excited to meet him. I heard the news when I was on my way back home from visiting Busch Gardens theme park in Williamsburg, Virginia, with my godmother Dorne and her cousins. When I met him, I immediately had a bond with him, and we have been close ever since.

From second to fifth grade I went back to attend P.S. 289. I always received awards and loved school. As a child, I was motivated to obtain an education and be successful. I wrote my goals and plans down all the time. I believed that if I could conceive it, I could achieve it. I had goals of going to college at ten years old after reading an article on successful students from HBCUs in Ebony magazine at Mama's house. I knew right away I needed to be an honor student. I saw that the children in the Special Progress (SP)/honor classes always were seen as the upper echelon and leaders of the school. Consequently, they were the students who received first pick when it came to receiving privileges and special opportunities. From second grade until fourth grade, I was in the second class in the grade, and I made it my goal to be in the honors class (first SP class) in fifth grade. It was in fifth grade that I met one of my best friends, Ebony B. I realized that my fifth grade teacher, Mrs. Toy definitely influenced me in a positive way. She pushed me and my entire class to become better students because we were the elite and we needed to understand that. Her name was Mrs. Toy, but she wasn't meant to be played with. When we attended school trips and school assemblies, she always commanded us to be on our best behavior since we represented her and the school. I was an honor student in the SP classes from fifth grade though the eighth grade.

I met my next best friend, Natasha, in the sixth grade. Our friends knew each other, but we became close when we went on a school trip to Washington, DC. None of my friends went on the trip, and I stayed with her and her mother, who brought the class a marble cake that was made by Natasha's grandmother, and that was the first time I ate a marble cake, and I loved it. To this day, marble cake is my favorite. Just as with Baria and Ebony B., I always loved Natasha and always will. In the seventh grade, I remember reading Romeo and Juliet in my honors English class. As a class assignment, we learned the play and performed it at another school in Brooklyn, I.S. 320 Jackie Robinson Intermediate School (junior high

school). I remember going to the school to per-
form it and seeing their principal, Sister
Mohammad. I later found out that Eddie attended
that school at the same time that I visited it with
my class. I always loved dancing and formed a
dance group with Baria, Ebony B., Baria's cousin
Ian, and our neighbor Devie. We went to dance
camp at Pratt Institute in the Clinton Hill section
of Brooklyn. We participated in a talent show and
came in second place. Outside of dancing, we
loved going to the Brooklyn Children's Museum,
which was a block away in our neighborhood.

Chrissy Becomes Chris
(1988–1992)—Christina's
POV

My second life-changing moment occurred when I was ten and my parents separated. My brothers and I had to adapt to my father not living with us. It was an uneasy feeling to experience my parents splitting up when that was all I had known. It was a major adjustment for all of us, especially my mother. Soon my mother got a job as a receptionist at a law firm in Manhattan. We stayed with babysitters after school, and when I was old enough, we were latchkey kids in the afternoons until my mother came home from work, and I took on the role of a second mother to my brothers. It was then we engrossed ourselves in watching movies that we were definitely too young for and probably shouldn't have been watching such as *Action Jackson, Predator, Aliens, Revenge of the Nerds, Trading Places, Coming to America, 10 to Midnight, The Best of Eddie Murphy's Saturday Night Live,* and a lot of Jean-Claude Van Damme and Steven Seagal's movies. Even now we love watching movies. My brothers and I grew closer because of those treasured moments. We called ourselves "ABC" for the first initials of our first names (Antonio, Brandon, and Chris).

In my eyes before my parents separated, they lived comfortable and isolated lives just spending time with family and close friends such as my godmothers, my godfather, and close neighbors. However, while my parents were separated, my mother met new friends and reconnected with old friends. Most of her new friends we met were single mothers that empowered and invigorated her. I also became empowered by being surrounded by so many strong women. I was motivated in 1988, at ten years old when I visited my godmother Shamean in Maryland because she was an independent young woman who graduated from Howard University. After visiting her, I was certain that I wanted to go college to ensure I would have a successful future. After three years of separation, my parents decided to get back together when I was thirteen years old, and they had another child, my little sister, Brianna. I learned who I really was in the summer of 1992, before I entered high school at the age of fourteen. I went to the Crown Heights Youth Collective in the Ebbets Field neighborhood to get my first summer youth job. I stood in a job line from morning until night in the hot sun. I did not have food or anything to drink for the entire time, and my parents could not find me and thought I was missing. My grandmother Ellen and her boyfriend found me at 10:00 p.m. and told me to go home, but I didn't receive my job assignment yet, and I told them I had to be assigned a job before I left, and that was the moment I learned I had determination and a drive to succeed.

I was really lucky to get my first summer job at the Brooklyn Children's Museum which was right in my neighborhood where all of my friends and I visited. My job at the museum was to assist visitors with interactive exhibits. I worked primarily in the toddler room for one to four years old. I would read them stories at designated reading times. I was so excited to get my first paycheck! It was also terrifying because we were required to pick up our checks from I.S. 320 (Eddie's former junior high school). The trouble was I.S. 320 was directly across the street from Ebbets Field (a housing development formerly Brooklyn Dodgers stadium). It was notorious for some of its residents robbing teenagers for their summer youth checks. I remember planning my strategy so that I had the quickest route back to the bus stop. I had to dress in a way to deter them from targeting me. They started handing out checks early in the morning every other Friday. I wore a Guess Jeans baseball cap, men's Guess Jeans shorts with long pockets (to hide my check) and sneakers in case I needed to run. Some residents would stalk the summer youth employees picking up their checks. They were standing within six feet of us. They sat on other people's cars waiting to follow us to the train or bus like a pack of wolves. They would intimidate us by saying they were going to rob us. The audacity of them to get up, dragging themselves out of bed to rob us for the checks we earned. There had to be hundreds of kids waiting for their checks. Many of the Ebbets Field residents were on bikes so they could grab someone's check and dash away quickly. I had to go into survival mode. You had to decide at that moment whether you were either a sheep or a wolf. I picked up my check and headed straight home. The next obstacle was cashing my check. Our payday cycles were known, so going to a check cashing store on payday should be avoided at all costs. After you cashed your check you also had to be on guard when you went shopping because that was the next obstacle. To prevent from being a target you had to guard your purchases with your life, get back on the train, or bus and head home. It was a perfect example of survival of the fittest. This cycle was repeated every two weeks until the end of the summer.

That fall of 1992, my father didn't want me to go to my zone school, Boys and Girls High School because he believed it wouldn't challenge me educationally, and so I registered at Canarsie High School. I didn't know until he recently informed me that he also did that because he didn't want me to follow his mistake. My father was a very smart child, and when he was in junior high, his teacher (who was a nun) told him he should apply to Edward R. Murrow High School in Brooklyn because it was one of the best schools for academics, but my father decided to go to Automotive High School so he could have a guaranteed job one day working with his hands. He said that decision changed his life because if he would have attended Edward R. Murrow, he probably would have gone on to college. My cousin also went to Canarsie High School. She was dating one of the football players, and she encouraged me to go out with the quarterback. How- ever, I didn't feel comfortable dating an older guy, and he knew that I was uncomfortable with our relationship; therefore, we stopped dating within two weeks, but I immediately became popular just because I was his girlfriend.

Canarsie High School was far from home for me. I had to take the C train from Crown Heights and then transfer to the L train to the last stop, then I walked a few blocks to school. I was incorrectly assigned to on-grade level Math, English, and History classes instead of honors. In my ninth grade English class, I read all the assigned texts in junior high school. I was so far ahead that I didn't have to study for the tests, and I knew the answers to all the questions the teacher posed to the class. I raised my hand for every question, and it annoyed the other students. I received A's and 100's on all exams. The teachers pulled me aside and told me that I didn't belong in their classes, and they were recommending me for honors (the highest for ninth grade). I told my teachers that I didn't belong there, but my guidance counselor needed a recommendation to move me to honors. Once I was reassigned to the correct class, I was moved to the honors homeroom. During my first week, I met a girl who was also a freshman named Tiffany, and she also took the L train since she lived in Brownsville, and we learned that we had many classes together. I met another girl who was also a freshman, Shanice, and we became friends. One day Shanice came into the lunchroom with a cute boy named Eddie, and I immediately liked him. One of the reasons I liked him was because to me he looked like a cross between the rapper Nas and Mr. Dalvin from the early 1990s R&B group Jodeci. I also met a girl in my English class who was dating a guy named Lewis, and soon I found out that he was very close friends with Eddie. One day I was walking to the train station with Tiffany, and we saw Lewis and Eddie, and again I immediately felt butterflies. I told Tiffany I wanted to ask Eddie out, but I was nervous because I didn't want to be rejected. We walked up to them at McDonald's, and while I stayed around twenty feet behind Tiffany, she asked Eddie out for me, and then he walked up to me, and we exchanged phone numbers.

Part Two: Two Lives Connect in High School (1992)

Eddie Meets Chris
(1992)—Eddie's POV

On October 9, 1992, Chris's and my lives changed forever. Me and Lewis walked Chris and Tiffany to the train station. We stopped in front of the train station, and Tiffany walked up to Lewis and me while Chris was around twenty steps behind her waiting. Tiffany stated, "So Eddie. My girl Chris wants to go out with you. What do you say?" I said, "Why didn't she come over and ask me?" She stated, "My girl is shy and nervous." I said, "Shy and nervous! Man, this is going to be hard!" I looked at Chris (just a straight beauty), then I said to Lewis, "I don't know, bro. Shorty looks like she'll be a hard one." He said, "Come on, man. I would if I was you. If you don't date her I sure will." I definitely didn't want him to be with her because he would have done her dirty, and if the relationship worked out, he would have rubbed it in my face every day. I told Tiffany, "Tell your girl I will go out with her." We all walked over to Chris, and she and I exchanged phone numbers, and they got on the train, and from that moment the way I felt about her changed. A few days later, we talked on the phone, and her voice was one in a million, and after a week or so, I met her after every class and walked her to her next class kissing and holding hands. We were comfortable with each other, and I was letting everyone know that she was mine. I realized I was falling for her especially when one day we were kissing, I walked her to the train station, and a guy we knew took a picture of us hugging (I still have that picture). I did not think she felt the same way, but she always did. The turning point and when I knew I was in love with her was the day she didn't come to school. One day in November, she had to stay home to watch her sister, and she didn't tell me she wasn't coming to school (we didn't have cell phones or beepers).

After I waited for her after two of her classes, I left school, went to the nearest pay phone, and called her because I was mad as hell. I said to her, "Chris! Why didn't you tell me you were staying home?" She said, "I'm sorry. I had to watch my little sister." I told her, "I missed you all morning, and I was running around waiting and looking for you. I'm just glad you didn't change schools on me." I always made sure I saw Chris in school, making sure I knew where to see her because it made my day. I even walked by her classes to make sure that she saw me, or I saw her. I remember one time while she was in the middle of her Spanish class, I knocked on the door and stated to the teacher, "Excuse me, but I need to give these roses to my wife." I walked over to Chris, handed her roses, kissed her on the cheek, and walked out of the classroom. All the students in the class looked amazed, and it was one of the smoothest actions I have ever done, and to this day

I bet everyone in that class remembers that moment. There we were in the beginning stages of being in love, and then out of nowhere, she turned off our love switch.

In early December, I cut class to spend time with Chris in the lunchroom while she was having lunch, then I walked her to her honors history class. Before she walked in, she had this worried look on her face, and I asked her what's wrong, and she stated, "I have to break up with you. My father said I can't have a boyfriend now because my grades are falling." She looked like she was about to cry, but I didn't believe her reason because I thought she wanted other guys because they had better clothes and because of what they could give her. Unfortunately, Fran died a week later, and Chris and I weren't together, but we saw and spoke to each other around and outside of school. However, in January, we became a couple again, and I went to Chris's sister Brianna's one year old birthday party. One time I visited Chris at her apartment, and her brothers wanted me to play karate with them while they threw punches and kicks at me, and they wanted me to play video games with them, and Chris called her mother to tell them to stop. Ironically, Chris lived around the corner and across the street from Ken (my godfather), and we never knew it. One day I told Chris I was going to my godfather's house and gave her the address, and she quickly told me he lived across the street from where she lived. She told me since she was a little girl, she and her family would see Ken and Jimmy (his long-time partner) sitting on their stoop and would exchange greetings. Big Eddie, Pete, and I visited Ken and Jimmy many times since they all enjoyed playing cards together, and we walked in front of Chris's home those times. Chris and I just missed seeing and/or meeting each other.

As teenagers (even sometimes as adults), we all have some kind of insecurity that hurts us in some way, and my insecurities were my clothes and lack of having any money. See, I didn't have money to buy the new Jordans, so I wore Timberlands instead (at the time they cost around seventy dollars). I didn't wear all the major clothing brands such as Polo or Tommy Hilfiger. I wore black and/or green fatigues instead because that was what most street guys wore, and they were in my price range. My insecurities made me question if Chris's love for me was for real (it really was, but I was stupid) because she broke up with me before, and to add to my worries, the majority of guys who traveled the same route she took home on the train had fly clothes and probably money. There were times when all she talked about was continuing to have fly name-brand clothes, and my mentality was "How was I supposed to know that she wouldn't break up with me again for one of those guys?" When everything between us was going great, in April (days after her birthday when I called her late around 9:00 p.m. while she waited by the phone), I broke up with her, and we never dated again. Days later, I asked her out, and even though she probably wanted to, she turned me down, and we both started down a road of dating miserably while she looked for someone like me and I looked for someone like her.

Amazingly, Chris was never permanently taken off the market. We talked on the phone occasionally, and we never asked each other out, but we both wanted to because the love was always there. I remember I visited her, and her mother said, "Ahh, don't worry. Y'all will get back together because you both are made for each other." I didn't think Chris cared for me anymore until one hot summer day Lewis and I visited Ken, and we unknowingly found out that Chris's parents were having a christening party for her sister, and Chris invited her friends and current boyfriend. Lewis and I stopped over there for a few minutes, and one of Chris's parents' friends' daughter was hitting on me, and although Chris and I weren't dating (just barely friends), she got mad at the girl. Lewis and I left and went back to Ken's house, and Chris and one of her best friends, Natasha, came over because Chris wanted to talk to me. They came in, and Chris stated, "Eddie! Please do not talk to that girl." I said, "Why? We're not together, and you don't love me anymore. What's the problem?" Lewis and Natasha left us, and Chris said to me, "Eddie, I love you. I will always love you. You will always be mine, and I will always be yours."

Anyone who knew us in high school or outside high school knew that we would somehow get back together (like in the movie *The Adjustment Bureau*). It was if somehow the people we dated knew the love Chris and I still had for each other. Her boyfriends in school knew their relationships only lasted as long as Chris and I kept playing games with each other. The same clowns who stared at us kissing in the hallways were the ones who ran to her "rescue." For some reason all those guys acted intimidated around me although I was shorter than them, perhaps it was the way I looked, I acted, or the monsters I was connected to, but guys never tried to play me with Chris (thanks to *God* and *Jesus Christ*).

I joined the football team my senior year as a backup wide receiver, and I went to camp for a week, and it was cool because I knew all the guys on the team, so I didn't get messed with during new players' hell week. I was doing great, but one of the starting receivers was a divo, and the coaches were afraid of him and only played me when there was a blowout. They knew he was out of control, and they planned to start me in the next couple of games. I still didn't have the hype gear since my day-to-day sneakers (low shell toe Adidas) were also the sneakers I practiced and played football in, so I would go home, and every night clean my sneakers for the next day. One day in practice, another player landed on my right leg, and the coaches stated I just twisted my ankle, so I trusted their judgment and decided to stay home because I could barely walk. However, after two days at home being in pain, I went to the hospital with Big Eddie, and we learned that I had a broken fibula, a broken tibia, and broken ankle. The injury left me out of physically attending school. I had a home tutor who provided me with eight classes, and the injury pushed my graduation out six months, so instead of graduating in fall 1996, I graduated in the spring of 1997. But in reality, I would not have graduated high school on time anyway, so breaking my leg was a blessing in disguise, and it showed me how much Chris still loved me. Once she heard what happened, she visited me.

Unfortunately, we stopped talking to each other because during our senior year, I told her last boyfriend she went on a date with me the day after the prom. She told him that I made up the whole thing because she didn't want to hurt him. She stopped talking to me until the last day of school because she was moving to Philadelphia to attend Temple University. Powerful (Chris's brother Tony) and his younger brother, Brandon, attended middle school a few blocks away from Canarsie High School. Their father didn't want them hanging with their friends from their neighborhood distracting them from their education, and he hoped they would follow Chris's successful academic career, so they also attended Canarsie High School. Powerful used to be with me all the time, and Big Eddie loved Powerful. Powerful used to stay nights at my house, and his mother stated it was fine as long as I watched over him. I used to tell Powerful, "You know I am going to marry Chris one day?" and he used to say, "I know, bro. Trust me, I know." When Chris was at Temple University, I used to ask her mother how Chris was doing, and I also told her that I would marry Chris, and she knew it too. Therefore, if I didn't break my leg on a routine practice play my senior year, and Powerful didn't attend Canarsie High School in the spring of 1997, I don't know how Chris and I would have connected at the right moment years later because he unknowingly became the connection between Chris and me

Chris Meets Eddie
(1992)—Christina's POV

When we started dating, everything was great, and I was excited because Eddie picked me up from the end of every class, and we held hands in the hallways before I went into my classes. We also met at the end of the school day and held hands while walking to the L Train. He waited until I got on the train or he rode with me to another train station. In the beginning, I felt shy around him because I still wasn't sure of the type of girl he liked. He definitely wasn't shy of showing his public displays of affection (PDA) toward me. He lived with his father, his father's best friend Pete, Pete's brother-in-law Chad. He didn't wear any brand name clothing like I did. He was clean, cute, and very popular. He always placed me first over his friends, he cared about my safety, and he never disrespected me. I had his pictures on a wall in my room, and I talked about him all the time to Baria, Ebony, and Natasha.

He surprised me from time to time (he still does) with flowers and giant balloons. Two times he entered my classes and asked my teachers if he could come in and give roses to his wife. We wrote each other love letters each day, and I would sign them "Mrs. Christina Sledge." I couldn't wait to meet him every day, but I broke his heart in the first week of December 1992, because my father told me that I was too emotionally involved with him, and my father didn't want my grades to fall. When I lost him, I thought we wouldn't ever get back together. He didn't believe that my father didn't want me to date him because I was too involved in our relationship. Eddie believed (he later told me years later) I was breaking up with him because he didn't have gold chains and brand name clothes. As he walked away, my butterflies stopped flying. I used to see Eddie around school, and he always made me smile since I always loved his smile, and he made sure that he spent time with me especially during my lunch and gym periods. I don't remember how it happened, but somehow, we just became a couple again. We were so much in love with each other that he became my first. We continued dating through junior year. We were one of the most well-known couples at school. I remember meeting TJ for the first time in my Chemistry class. She and I hit it off because we had a bunch in common. We both had the same Tommy Hilfiger jacket, hers was navy blue and mine was red. We also wore similar Panamanian jewelry. We later found out that we were distant cousins on my father's side. She and I hung out every day before and after school. Valentine's Day was the only day TJ and I didn't hang out together. It was a big deal for couples at school, guys seemed to unofficially compete to buy their girlfriends the biggest and most balloons and gifts. Eddie always showed off with lots of gifts for me.

On my sixteenth birthday, things changed; he didn't call me until 9:00 p.m. and picked a fight with me on the phone, and a few days later, he broke up with me while we were in school. I hated him for that. I was heartbroken, and I couldn't understand what I did wrong or where our relationship went wrong. I thought maybe he got tired of me, but I never realized until after we married that he felt insecure that he didn't have the brand name clothing. I would have bought Eddie clothes if he wanted them, but looking back, I should have just bought them for him. I started going out with other boys in school, but those relationships didn't last for more than a few months. When I dated other boys, Eddie called me to check on me, and there were times when he picked me up from my after school job late at night and took me home just to make sure that I was safe. I remember when I learned that Eddie broke his leg when he was on the football team, and even though we weren't dating and didn't talk to each other for a while, my first reaction was "Who, my Eddie?" I visited him to see how he was doing, and he gave me his football jersey. I was not dating anyone at the time. That was one of the several times we should have gotten back together, but I told him no because I was still hurt that he broke up with me. I didn't want him to think he could do that to me again.

Eddie Without Chris
(1996–1999)—Eddie's POV

In early June 1998, I was in an extremely bad place in my life since I wasn't working and I had a baby on the way, struggling day to day, and hanging around people for bus fare. I had to find a way to get on my feet and out of the projects. I accepted a job as a warehouse collector for a major supermarket chain, and I was paid thirteen dollars per hour, and my hours were 3:00 p.m. to 11:00 p.m. I rode a bike through a couple of neighborhoods, and I got home in around thirty minutes. My duties included riding a forklift around a huge warehouse, picking out items from a manifest, placing them on a pallet, wrapping it up, and loading it on a long trailer so it could be delivered to several supermarkets. My manager was a young Jamaican guy named Roger, and he wore a lot of skinny gold chains (looked like the Mr. T's starter kit). None of the employees wore uniforms, and they were either young men who were fast at their jobs or slow old men who had worked there between fifteen and twenty years. One day while I was working, one of my older black male coworkers said to me, "Young man. What are your goals?" I said, "To continue to work here for a long time. This job isn't bad at all." He provided me with some of the best advice I ever was provided. He said, "You see Roger over there? He doesn't have to put any wear and tear on his body because of his position. He's young, has a great car (a cherry-colored two-door Lexus), and he isn't stuck at this place because he can go almost anywhere. As for me and the rest of us, we're stuck here doing this backbreaking work, and do you know the reason he is there, and we are here? Because he has a college degree, and every day I wished I got a college degree. Young man, don't make the huge mistake of not going to college and getting a degree because young blood, you will regret it." Weeks later I quit my job, but I wasn't motivated to go to college, I just continued looking for another job hanging in the streets.

A life-changing moment in my life came in November 1998. I went to visit my family in Maryland for a few days (I don't remember the city), and I hung out with my two older male cousins from Fran's family. The oldest was a tall, skinny, dark-skinned guy named Greg, and he had it together. He had a nice new townhome, a new Nissan Maxima, and a beautiful wife. One night we were driving around the city, and I said to him, "Bro. You got your shit together. Put me on with what you're doing?" He said to me, "Bro. I got all this because I joined the navy and took advantage of the benefits, then I got a job at the post office. That's how you do it." Usually when a street guy asks another street guy to put him on, it involves some kind of illegal activity, but Greg dropped one of the illest jewels on me. Therefore, I knew I was joining the military, but I learned that I had to pass the Armed Services Vocational Aptitude Battery (ASVAB) test, and I had to study hard.

Two days after I returned to Brooklyn, I went to the air force recruiter station, which was right next to the army recruiter station. I talked to the air force recruiter, and he told me the score I needed to pass the ASVAB, so for weeks I studied, and I set a date to take the test. The majority of people I knew hated that I was joining the military because they wanted me to stay, but they didn't understand what I was mentally going through. I was broke and had a baby on the way, and in the streets my only options were either be killed or sit in prison; I was facing rock bottom. I wasn't coming back to Brooklyn. I knew guys in Brooklyn who joined the military, came back, and lived in the projects working jobs they didn't like. I didn't want my story to be one of those, so I had to make it out and stay out. At that time Chris was at Temple and lived in the rough part of Philadelphia. She was dating a tall, light-skinned guy named Trey, but he cheated on her, and they broke up but eventually returned to each other. Since Chris and I broke up in high school, neither of us had found our perfect match, and she kept looking, and I stopped looking. There were two times when we saw each other while in relationships with other people, but we didn't do anything even though we should have, which would have changed our lives. The first time was during her freshman year when she came over to my apartment, and the second time was in the summer of 1998 when we saw each other at the Greek Picnic in Philadelphia. To this day, Chris tells me that we should have spent time together, but she was still with Trey, but it wasn't meant to be at that time. Those missed opportunities probably would not have worked out for us since we had to live our lives to avoid huge relationship mistakes with each other like the several couples we later would meet.

The first Tuesday of December around 8:00 a.m., I arrived at the air force recruiter station ready to go; however, thirty minutes went, and the recruiter didn't show up. So, then the army recruiter showed up and started opening his location. He looked at me and stated, "You waiting for him, uh? You can wait in here with me and the heat." I went inside, then he asked me why the air force, told me what the army can provide me, and showed me pictures of his four cars and also pictures with a few New York Knicks players. I was feeling him. I passed the ASVAB, I signed up, and then as soon as I walked out, I saw the air force recruiter, and he stated to me, "What's up, buddy? Are you ready?" The army recruiter came out, looked at him, and said, "We got him. I will take care of him."

That was a key moment because if I had the patience to wait, what would have been the odds that the next year I would have the opportunity to meet up with Chris? I probably would've been stationed out of the United States and/or married another woman. On New Year's Eve 1998, Big Eddie threw me a going away party with his friends, my friends, and several of our closest family members who all came and partied. Honestly, I had to leave Brooklyn because I felt it was just a matter of time when I would've got caught doing something dumb and sent to prison because I either tried to protect myself, did something to build my street rep, or worst, I would've been killed by someone I did dirty. I was always pushing the envelope, and I didn't understand that *God* and *Jesus Christ* were keeping me from a dangerous moment so I would become Chris's husband.

Eddie Joins the Army
(1999)—Eddie's POV

On January 6, 1999, around 1:00 p.m., I grabbed my bags and walked into Big Eddie's room and gave him a giant hug, and he cried (the only other time I saw him cry was the night Fran died). He wanted me to go and make something of myself, but he needed me to stay, and that was a rough moment between the both of us because we had become best friends. I remember when I was a child, he used to tell me to join the army and make a career out of it, and I was taking the first step toward that. My plan was to get my life together and provide for my daughter. I hurt a lot of people by leaving because I wasn't going to be there for them anymore; however, one of the greatest things I have done in my life was join the army. I rode the local bus to the recruiter office, and he drove me to Fort Hamilton Army Base in Brooklyn. I did my paperwork, and around 6:00 p.m. other enlistees and I went to a hotel in New Jersey for a few hours.

I met a young black guy from Brooklyn who had enlisted in the marines, and we went into a hotel room that had a few enlistees playing cards. I remember a dark-skinned, tall, medium-size brother named Bus, a light-skinned, tall Puerto Rican guy from the Bronx named Delgado, and a small, medium-complexioned brother from

Brooklyn named Jermaine. After a few hours, since we all were heading to Ft. Sill, Oklahoma, we agreed we would hold each other down, especially since Jermaine was a small, timid, and soft-spoken brother. As a side note, Jermaine reached out to me on Facebook (when I was on it a few years ago), and he wasn't a small and timid brother anymore. My man was built like a rock, and he told me that without me, Bus, and Delgado holding him down, he would have never made it and never would have gained confidence, and that was great news to hear. Soon all of the enlistees gathered our bags and took a bus to JFK airport, and that was the day the NBA players ended their lockout (when Michael Jordan left the NBA for the second time), and the union players were in New York. So, the four of us sat together, and around 8:00 p.m. we loaded onto the plane heading to Dallas since it was my first flight ever, and I was sitting right next to NBA legend Sam Perkins. He looked at me and said, "Hey, little man. Whatever you do, don't throw up on me." We talked during the whole flight while he explained all the good, the bad, and the dirty players in the league, then we landed in Dallas, and Bus, Jermaine, Delgado, and I got off and received different hotel rooms.

In the morning, we met at Dallas airport and took a quick flight to Oklahoma (I thought Oklahoma was a city in Nebraska), and from that flight, we took a small eight-seat plane heading to the town of Lawton. The plane ride was extremely scary since the plane was leaning toward the side with the most weight, and I think we didn't even go above the clouds (we all were scared to death). We got off the plane and walked through an empty and tiny bootleg airport with a few small, fragile looking Native American women whom we exchanged greetings with (my first time ever seeing or speaking to one). It was around 12:00 p.m. in early January, cold and gloomy, and I said to myself, "What the hell am I doing here? My recruiter didn't tell me about this!" From the airport we drove to the army base, got our introduction to our new world, went to our temporary barracks, received, and changed into our uniforms, and went to eat chow (which means either breakfast, lunch, or dinner). The next morning when we entered the chow hall, we noticed around thirty soldiers eating, all looking at us like we were fresh meat in jail, and I told Bus, "Bro. Get ready to knuckle up with these dudes." He agreed especially since we didn't know what was about to go on. Later that day we and other new soldiers received medical shots, and one of the shots was a painful shot in one of our buttocks. Five soldiers at a time lined up facing the wall with their pants down to their ankles while a female soldier squeezed each soldier's left buttock and provided the shot. I was in the second group, and in the group before me, there was a tall and skinny soldier from Hawaii who took the shot and quickly started shaking and urinating. I think the nurse hit a nerve and the soldier reacted. Again, I thought what the hell am I doing here?!

After our shots, we were sore, and unfortunately, I slept on the top bunk, so my ass was hurting for days! A few days later, we finally saw some of the soldiers who were eating chow, and we came to find out they were new like us. As a matter of fact, they arrived two days before we did, and a few of them saw us like we saw them with the "knuckle up" attitude. After talking with them, we became cool since most of us knew that the army was just a jump-off for our livelihoods. The first three weeks were the worst since we all had to break out of our old ways of thinking just to get through basic training. I met a lot of soldiers who entered the army to escape the life of selling drugs, facing prison, or just putting food on the table. There were a few soldiers who were true GI Joes, a few who shouldn't have been there but were there proving a point to their well-to-do families who spoiled them throughout their childhood and teenage years, and one or two soldiers who couldn't even put their uniforms on correctly (what the hell?). I knew that the army was only a job and that I couldn't afford to fail at it because this was my opportunity to grow and never turn back, and thanks to *God* and *Jesus Christ*, I made it but not without a lot of bumpy moments because basic training will test you physically and mentally.

I remember the first night in our permanent barracks, and the drill sergeants had worked us all day in the cold and wet grass, so we were wet, nasty, and dirty. One of our four drill sergeants yelled, "Everyone! It's time to make your buddy smile. Shower time!" I looked at Bus and said, "What the hell he's talking about. This doesn't sound good." Another drill sergeant poured a quarter size amount of liquid soap in each soldier's hand and stated that for the first three weeks all soldiers will only be allowed to take fifteen-second showers. So, I was standing there close as hell behind the soldier in front of me, butt naked covering my crotch with one hand and soap in the other, then running into the showers trying to get clean in fifteen seconds! What in the hell am I doing here?! Since there were only eight showers and around thirty soldiers living in our barracks, other soldiers were yelling at the soldiers to get out of the showers, and those moments led to yelling matches, frustration, and Tuesday night fights. Then for the first few weeks around 5:00 a.m., drill sergeants came through yelling, cursing, and kicking over metal garbage cans, waking us up. Then we wore these thin sweats and hoodies doing physical training (PT) in about ten-degree weather, I was cold as hell feeling like my hands and feet were about to break off. What in the hell am I doing here?! I remember training outside one day when it was so cold that even the drill sergeants had to train us inside because we barely could feel any of our limbs. Then because we all had to pass at least four PT tests, we were "encouraged" into not eating what we really wanted to eat, during chow the drill sergeants laughed and stated something like, "Watch it, soldier. You eat that beautiful tasty chocolate cake and you won't pass your PT test, and you will have to do remedial PT or start basic training all over again."

Sometimes the army reminded me of some of the stories I heard from guys who did time in prison. Soldiers got mad when you stayed too long on the phone, snitched on other soldiers, and verbally and physically disrespected soldiers, leading to Tuesday night fights. Tuesday night fights (actually it was any night) were when two soldiers went inside the bathroom (with soldiers watching and one watching the main door), and the two fought it out. This never happened in our barracks, but we knew that it happened in others, and we believed the drill sergeants knew it too. One day a tall, skinny, white soldier from Louisiana called black soldiers in his battery monkeys, and a tall, built (physically intimidating), real hardcore soldier beat the crap out of him during Tuesday night fights. The next day the white soldier had black eyes and a busted lip, and one drill sergeant stated to him, "What the hell happened to you, soldier?" The soldier stated, "I fell down the stairs." Another drill sergeant stated, "Stop lying! You got your ass whooped, soldier!" Of course, sometimes you cannot wait for Tuesday night fights.

There was another soldier from Brooklyn who always rebelled against any soldier who was the leader of a certain training; he used to say, "I'm not doing that." One day I was given the leader's duties of having our barracks cleaned (mopped and waxed), and I gave him the task of mopping, and I was ready for his response since I knew it would be something disrespectful. He stated, "Yeah right. I ain't doing that." I said "Soldier! You will do this task that I gave you!" We started yelling at each other, and then for a brief moment I lost it. I ran up to him, wrapped my hands around his neck, and held him against the window. After soldiers broke us up, the drill sergeants made us battle buddies (we were each other's right-hand man), and we became associates. The army provided several great memorable moments in my life, and unfortunately one was the gas chamber, and that really sucked! Since the first week of basic training, we were told by drill sergeants and a few regular active duty soldiers about the gas chamber, and many of us circled that day on our calendars (ironically my recruiter didn't tell me about that crap, which he had to go through once a year). So, the day finally arrived, and we did a long road march to the building and arrived there around 12:00 p.m. We stopped and sat down right across the street from the gas chamber. We ate our nasty meals ready to eat (MREs), and after we ate, we entered the gas chamber. It had a strange eerie feeling.

The outside looked like a plain gray cement-block building about ten feet tall, and inside it consisted of two large rooms separated by a wall and a metal door, and the door had a small 5" x 5" window (so soldiers could see and become mentality messed up). There were close to forty of us. We were divided into five groups, and I think they let in eight at a time, which were four sets of battle buddies, and I was part of the second group, so we were looking through the window. The first group entered with their masks on, and they all stood on a line with their backs toward us, and the chemical gas sergeant was cooking the gas that filled the room, but he wasn't wearing his mask, so we said it couldn't be that bad (but he was used to it). Then we saw the soldiers take off their masks, and all hell broke loose. Quickly soldiers were coughing and throwing up, and all tried at one point to run toward the back door that was straight ahead of them. We couldn't hear anything, but we were scared, and less than five minutes later it was our turn. We walked in with our masks on, and all the sergeants were standing there with smiles on their faces and a few with vomit on their boots. Then we were told to take our masks off, and as soon as we did, we started coughing. It felt like my face was literally set on fire, my throat like I had drunk Drano, my eyes sprayed with five times the amount of mace. We were told that to leave we had to say our full names, our social security numbers, our ranks, and our battle buddy's same information. I barely finished my information, but my battle buddy (a young Mexican soldier from Texas) couldn't finish fast enough, so I threw up on one of my drill sergeants' boots. Finally, my battle buddy finished, and we ran out the door, and once the air hit my face, all the feelings were ten times worse because those nasty MREs continued coming up rough. One soldier ran into a tree and almost knocked himself out, and everyone had snot falling from our noses and it took all of us a long time to recoup.

One day I called Big Eddie, and Powerful was there, and he gave me Chris's address even though she was with Trey. That night while I was on guard duty (a two-hour night shift watching over the soldiers while they slept), I wrote Chris a letter explaining my army experiences and that I had a daughter on the way. I really didn't think she would care or even open my letter because I thought she was probably getting married. She wrote me back and explained how she was having a rough time in their relationship and that she always loved me. We continued writing to each other, and she stated that Trey knew about one of my letters and became mad at her. In March, Big Eddie and Eleanor came, stayed in a hotel, and saw me walk across the stage as I graduated basic training, and it was one of the proudest moments of our lives. I loved Eleanor because she was a great woman to me and a great fit for Big Eddie. After basic training, I spent four weeks in Advanced Individual Training (AIT), and after I graduated, I stayed at Big Eddie's house for a week, and during the second day I met my daughter for the first time. She was one of the reasons I was motivated to become a better man.

In July 1999, I arrived at Ft. Stewart 3rd Infantry Division in Georgia (around forty-five minutes from Savannah), and it was (still is) a heavy mechanized base, and that meant that it was the first to be called for war because of its tanks and many battalions. I was assigned to a Field Artillery section and to one of the two Fire Direction Center (FDC) sections because the FDC was (still is) the brains of Field Artillery (as a matter of fact, my section won top FDC for the entire base my first year there). Here's how the FDC works with the other sections and units to fight the enemy. On the battlefield, Infantry soldiers locate the enemy, they call FDC and provide the location of the enemy, then the FDC finds where the enemy is on a map and makes sure friendly units aren't nearby. The FDC determines what missiles are best to use on the enemy, then it informs the soldiers in the tanks where and which missile to shoot, and when the tanks are ready, FDC informs each tank when to shoot. In my section, it was me and three cool white soldiers who included my squad leader, a tall, young, crazy Italian from New Jersey who we called chief (the head sergeant of a section), and he stood by his soldiers especially when we faced any kind of discipline, and I loved that guy.

In less than two weeks from arriving, we deployed to the Mojave Desert in California, and it had some of the most beautiful morning skies I have ever seen especially when they were light purple. Since I was the lowest-rank soldier in my section, I automatically received the craziest and dirtiest duties such as trash and kitchen duties, which both sucked especially in the desert or field (woods). As the lowest-ranking soldier in the section, I also had to sleep outside with the wild animals on a used cot. My first night was very cold. I slept in my uniform and placed my boots under my sleeping bag, using them as a pillow, which also kept the bugs and snakes out of my boots. I slept outside next to the rear of our tank, and my feet were near the full, closed, hanging trash bag. Around 2:00 a.m. I heard a wild boar and her babies tearing up the trash bag and one of my bags, and while they were doing that, I was quiet, I stayed still, and I prayed that they wouldn't bother me. What the hell am I doing here?! In the morning, trash was all over the place, and my half gallon of grape Kool-Aid powder had holes punched in it. We received two hot meals per day while out in the desert (also when we were in the field), and sometimes we would be so far out that the hot chow (breakfast and dinner) would be cold as hell, and without protection from the outside elements, a sandwich really turned into a real SANDwich. I remember one time, because of an unexpected sandstorm, I wiped sand off my cold food so I could eat for the night. Daytime was an extremely hot time, and I hated it. I remember there were snake holes everywhere, and there weren't any showers; therefore, all soldiers (men and women) made the best of it. Many sections stood up several cots in the sand for cover, used a portable shower hanging from the back of a tank, stood on a cardboard box, and took a shower or instead used baby wipes. What the hell am I doing here?!

When soldiers took off their uniforms and changed into their civilian clothing, we saw who they really were. I knew good soldiers who just kept to themselves and husbands who just went straight home and tried to provide for their families with very low salaries the best they could. However, I also knew soldiers young and older who were total opposite. There was adultery, domestic violence (from both parties because I even saw two male soldiers with black eyes from their wives), robberies, drug and alcohol abuse, baby mama drama, divorces - you name it and it was part of many soldiers' personal lives. I was told by my staff sergeant the reason I was selected to my section was because I took the place of one of the two soldiers who were arrested for robbery and murder. I hung out with soldiers from different parts of America and from around the world, and mostly all of them were from poor urban areas and loved rap and hip hop. We embraced some of the same rappers. Soldiers from the Midwest loved Biggie and Nas, while soldiers from the west coast loved Biggie, Nas, and Jay-Z, and I dug some of their music but mostly Chicago rappers such as Kanye West and Twista.

I had to get my driver's license because I was the lowest-ranked soldier in my section, I had to be the driver of our tank, and also if you didn't have a car, you were looked down upon. I used to watch people drive, but I never paid attention to their feet (I couldn't see what they were doing). One day my man took me to the Georgia Motor Vehicle Department to take my written and road tests, and the officer sat in the passenger seat and told me to check my mirrors and lights and start the car. I did all of that, then he instructed me to reverse out of the parking space, and I couldn't do it. I tried to move the stick, but I didn't know that I needed to place my foot on the brake. After two minutes of not moving the car, the officer told me to go inside and get my driver's permit. I returned to base and told my chief, and he told me to place my foot on the brake to move the car, and I went back the next day, got my driver's license, and a few weeks later, bought my first car. I wanted the white 1995 Lexus ES350, but it was a stick (thanks to *God* and *Jesus Christ*, in 2015 I bought a new white Lexus ES350), and plus I didn't have any credit. Credit is like having a little dirt on you because without it, businesses won't trust you; therefore, I bought a black 1991 Chrysler New Yorker with 175,000 miles. It had butter-soft cloth material and a lot of room in the front and back. I drove off the lot feeling like a champ.

Around that time, I barely talked with any of my friends back in Brooklyn, and when I did, I learned that their lives went on without me, and that hurt me, and they probably felt the same way. Big Eddie told me that my daughter was left with him and Eleanor for weeks at a time. Soon, Big Eddie and I went to court to get full custody. I went to Brooklyn, and Big Eddie, Powerful, and I went to court, and the judge found in my favor. Since I was a single parent in the army, the judge would not let me have physical custody; therefore, my daughter lived with Big Eddie.

Chris Without Eddie
(1996–1999)—Christina's POV

I was ahead of the honors class curriculum until eleventh grade. Once I went to eleventh grade, my teachers recommended me for Advanced Placement (AP) English, History, and Precalculus. I was so advanced there were times I didn't go to class and still got A's on all the tests and assignments. Seeking higher education was my chosen path to success, and I knew that was the ticket to the future I wanted. I was determined to go to a university. I began applying to universities in the fall of my senior year of high school. I and several other seniors from my honors homeroom met with our guidance counselor to complete applications for universities and apply for financial aid and scholarships. I applied to several schools with Temple University being my first choice. I had several extracurricular activities, I was vice president of my senior class, a cheerleader / booster, a peer counselor, and a member of the sorority at our school. I also worked a part-time job at a local shoe store in downtown Brooklyn at Albee Square Mall, and at a grocery store in the Park Slope section of Brooklyn as a cashier after school in the summers of my junior and senior years to earn money. I made sure my application was marketable, and I was so excited when I was accepted to Temple University.

Senior year, I was asked out by a boy named Emerson who went to our school. Eddie knew him from the projects. We started dating but I think he knew there was a great chance that Eddie and I would get back together. I went to the prom with Emerson and the next night Eddie called me to go to the movies. Two days later, Eddie got into a dispute with Emerson because Eddie bragged about going out on a date with me a few nights earlier to spite Emerson. Eddie and I got into an argument about it. Looking back on it, I don't know why we played those games and didn't just get back together. After that, Eddie and I didn't speak to each again until the last day of school as I was getting ready for the summer before I went to Temple University.

I was the first in my immediate family to go to a university and graduate; however, the beginning of my college and young adult years started rough. I excelled academically in the classroom at Temple, but I struggled outside the classroom adjusting to life. I underestimated the emotional and mental support I needed to be successful in my early adulthood. I felt extremely alone during this time. I also had to deal with living in a new environment. I was originally planning to live on Temple University's beautiful suburban campus located in Ambler, Pennsylvania; however, we missed the deadline for the housing deposit, and I had to live on the main campus in North Philly. In August of 1996, my parents drove me to Philly and dropped me off. We wiped away tears as I embarked on my new journey. It was through this experience that I realized everything happens for a reason. I learned that things may not align the way you expect, but you can learn something from every experience. During my first few weeks at Temple, Emerson and I broke up because of the long distance. At Temple, I met a guy from Philly, Trey. He was tall and attractive. We began dating shortly after we met. I got a work study job to help support myself. I was slowly pushed into depending on Trey for emotional support, and I knew that wouldn't turn out well for me especially since he had his own problems. I had no one else in my life who I could have turned to for either emotional and financial support except for Mama and my closest friends, but I didn't want to be a burden on them.

That year before Christmas break, Trey drove me to Brooklyn. After break, Trey picked me up and took me back to Philly. By allowing Trey to do that, I self-consciously became dependent on Trey, and he knew it. I continued to work, and I changed jobs as I worked for an event reservationist at the Student Activity Center on campus, as her assistant. My predecessor, Anthony, was leaving his position and recommended me for the job. Janice and I hit it off well; she was petite, and an Aries like me. During the summer break, all the students who lived in the dorms had to move out. Therefore, I got a job as a student orientation counselor, and by doing that, I wouldn't have to move out of the dorms and could have food to eat for free. I knew one of the student orientation counselors, Ebony C., who was also a freshman since we had classes together, and we met another girl, Nikki who was also a freshman from Boston.

In 1998, in my junior year I was tired of living in the dorms, and my financial aid had decreased so I could no longer afford room and board, so I moved out and moved in with Nikki and her roommate. However, Nikki was soon moving in with her boyfriend, so I found and rented an apartment in North Philly, and it was less than fifteen minutes away from school. It was surrounded by drugs, pimps, prostitutes, poverty, abandoned buildings, and dark alleys. I walked home every day and night not knowing what would happen to me. I walked in front of a brothel every night since it was a block down from where I lived. Looking back on it, I have to thank *God* that I successfully survived living there. I worked three student jobs at the computer lab, the student movie theater at the ticket booth, and as a projectionist on alternate days. That was only enough to pay my four hundred dollars a month rent, electricity, and phone bills. I spent many nights hungry just eating crackers and drinking water. I was literally a starving student during that year. How- ever, I knew by staying in school, I definitely would become successful. The situation was tough because I worked so hard in school to avoid living in those kinds of places. I leaned on Mama and my best friend, Natasha, and started seeing a school therapist to support me mentally and emotionally during the rough times.

To top everything off, I found out Trey was cheating on me. I had my suspicions, and I ignored the signs. He was never a good fit for me, but I struggled with low self-esteem at that time in my life, and he became my emotional support. When we first started dating, I noticed a few times when he spoke to girls, he was just too friendly, while I watched him from a distance and ignored my suspicions. He was using me as a novelty because he never had a girlfriend from Brooklyn, so he would tell his friends and show me off just to say he had been to Brooklyn and he dated a girl from Brooklyn. He blinded and lied to me and at the same time he supported me. He bought me expensive gifts and told me he loved me. He also had a lot of personal issues. He was an alcoholic, and he constantly drank. He used to walk around with a quart of cheap vodka mixed with cheap juice drinking it all day. He passed out several times while on the phone with me at night, and one time he was so drunk that he called me and said he couldn't drive home, so he slept in his car in an unknown area. I had nightmares that he was cheating on me, and when I asked him, he gaslighted me and said I was crazy, but I knew deep down he was, then his aunt finally told me that he was cheating on me, and that confirmed it. In an email, she told me that he brought girls over to her house. We broke up but still dated off and on again while I dated other guys. My self-esteem was so low that I continued to be with him.

I needed to snap out of the self-esteem rut I was in. In July 1998, an amazing thing happened, I went with a few girls to the annual Greek Picnic that was held in Philly, and while I was there, I ran into Eddie. Wow! We hadn't seen each or talked to each other in a couple years, and in front of everyone he ran up to me and hugged and picked me up, and we took a picture. He didn't care who I was with since he stood there holding my hand, and he told me that he knew I would be there and he would see me, and the girls I was with asked me who he was, and I told them he was my high school sweetheart. I wished we spent more time together that day. That was another perfect moment we could have gotten back together. In February 1999, I received a letter from Eddie when he was in the army, and soon Trey found out about it. I was still in love with Eddie, and I even visited him once while I was dating Trey. When he saw the letter, Trey asked me, "Do you still love him?" I said, "Of course. He's my first love." I didn't care about Trey anymore since our relationship was damaged.

I thought about Eddie often because I knew he would never cheat on me and treat me the way Trey did, but in his letter, Eddie stated that he was having a baby and things were not working out with her mother. I thought about the times we could have gotten back together and started our lives together. I thought it was over for me and Eddie. I continued to be in an off-and-on relationship with Trey in 1999 and dated other guys. I knew I deserved better, so on December 22, 1999, I got down on my knees and prayed to *God* to send me a good man who would treat me right, and the *Lord* answered my prayer.

The same day, I went to Brooklyn because I was on Christmas break from school, and my mother told me that Eddie was also in Brooklyn on his Christmas break from the army and he was hanging out with my brother Tony. Tony went to Canarsie High School the year after I graduated, and because Eddie broke his leg in his senior year, he had to wait another six months to graduate. Eddie and Tony knew each other since Tony was ten years old because Eddie used to visit me when we were and sometimes when we weren't dating, and my family liked Eddie. Since I started college, my mother used to tell me that Eddie would tell her to tell me hello. I hadn't seen Eddie since the Greek Picnic. Eddie, Tony, and their friend Rich came to my parents' house, and I realized at that moment that I still loved him, but I didn't think there was any future for us. He said he had things to do during the week and that he would come stop by and see me in a couple days for us to hang out, and I was excited because ever since the Greek Picnic, I knew we should have been together. Eddie came over to my parents' house again to visit me a couple days later. I was nervous and could feel the butterflies again. When he picked me up (it was December 24, 1999), he had a black Chrysler New Yorker, and it was roomy and clean inside. That impressed me because he didn't have a sports car like a lot of guys his age, and it showed he had style and the boy I had known became a man. It was cold, and we tried to think of places to go, and he suggested that we go to Big Eddie's apartment so he could introduce me to his daughter.

While there, Big Eddie asked me, "If Eddie asked you to marry him, what would you say?" I told him yes, I would, but I was thinking that would be years later, so I thought nothing of it. We spent a few hours together, and Eddie asked me to marry him, and I told him yes, but didn't think he was serious. I thought it was something he just said to keep me with him after all those years. However, it felt special since our engagement was on Christmas Eve, and Christmas is my favorite holiday. I knew he was the man *God* sent to me answering my prayer. A few days later, I left to go back to Philly. I came back to Brooklyn before New Year's Eve (NYE) to spend it with Eddie. Eddie began introducing me as his fiancée, and I said to myself, he is serious, and this is real. On

NYE, we celebrated together at Big Eddie's. Eddie proceeded to tell me about the complications of his custody battle. While he was driving, I was at a crossroads with two options. I thought to myself, do I let him take me home to my parents' house and tell him that we cannot be engaged, and by doing that, I would lose the only man I loved, wondering if we could have made it work, and return to Philly hoping to find Mr. Right even though Eddie was who I prayed for, so I knew he was for me. My other option was to stay with him and take on the potential challenges ahead and hopefully things between them would get better. I decided to stay with Eddie because I knew he loved me, and *God* gave me the answer I needed. It was one of the best decisions I ever made.

The next day, we went to breakfast and talked about our plans for a wedding, then I told Natasha, Ebony B., and my family that we were engaged, and they were happy for me. When I got back to Philly, I told my friends from Temple that I was engaged, and they were shocked because I never talked about Eddie to them and Trey and I were off and on. I informed the guys I was dating (including Trey). Trey instantly knew that it was Eddie I was engaged to. Trey had the audacity to tell me he planned to propose to me on my birthday and bought a ring and everything. I told Trey it was too late. Eddie and I talked on the phone every day, and I felt like I was living in a dream. I couldn't believe we got back together and were getting married just like that. On Dr. Martin Luther King Jr. 's birthday, Eddie had a four-day weekend, and he drove up from Georgia to spend the long weekend with me. He arrived on a Friday morning, and we spent three magical days together. It was like a dream. All those love letters in high school when we talked about getting married were actually coming true. We went places and held hands. I loved the entire time together because he made me feel special. He left at 6:00 a.m. Monday morning to go back to Georgia. We talked every day on the phone after that.

Two weeks went by, and I was struggling financially since I was in school full-time as a computer science major; it was now even more difficult to work enough hours to pay the rent and balance my classes. One night, Eddie called me and said his chief and captain would give him a few days off for him to come to Philly so we could be married, and he even sang Jagged Edge's song "Let's Get Married" on the phone to me. We knew we could not afford the big Christmas wedding we planned and wanted that year. However, I researched what we had to do, and I found out that February 18, 2000, was the best date because it was in the middle of the provided time frame that Eddie was given leave. We would have a couple days after to spend together.

Eddie arrived on Sunday, which was Valentine's Day. On Monday we went to the courthouse, paid for our marriage license, and completed the paperwork needed for us to get married. There was a mandatory three-day waiting period in Pennsylvania before a marriage could take place. During the process, I couldn't believe that it was actually happening, and I was nervous, but Eddie was excited. We needed a witness, and our closest friends weren't able to come to Philly because it was short notice. Our plan was to elope privately and then hopefully have a big wed- ding eventually. I didn't tell anyone in my family including my parents because I knew my father would be disappointed if he couldn't walk me down the aisle. Therefore, I asked Ebony C. to be our witness and she agreed, but she questioned if I should be getting married since I just came out of a relationship with Trey. And out of nowhere I was now marrying Eddie, who she never met and never heard me talk about. I told her and my other friends that he was my first love, my high school sweetheart, and the only man I ever loved.

The morning of February 18, I woke up ready to be married and to start my life as Mrs. Sledge, since that was the name I wrote at the end of my love letters to Eddie in high school. Eddie was so excited and couldn't wait to marry me. We planned to be at the wedding chapel at 2:00 p.m. We picked up Ebony C. around 1:00 p.m., and since we couldn't afford to buy me a wedding gown or rent a tuxedo for Eddie, I wore my cream-colored prom dress and he wore his army class-A uniform. The wedding chapel was located on the first floor of a row house in South Philly, and after we exchanged greetings and information with the minister, he married us in less than thirty minutes. When we were leaving, Eddie carried me over the snow and into the car, we dropped Ebony C. off at her house, and Eddie called Big Eddie and told him that we just got married, and he and Eleanor (Big Eddie's longtime girlfriend) sent us fifty dollars through Western Union as a congratulations gift. We picked up the money, went to KFC (our first meal as a married couple), and went back to my apartment. I thought wow, we just got married!

Still in Love
1999 Eddie's POV

A week before Thanksgiving, a few soldiers and I went to a club and almost got into a fight. A few days later, I was sitting in my room when my first sergeant came and told me that since I got in trouble, he could not grant me my Thanksgiving leave, and I had to walk a straight line if I wanted to keep my Christmas leave. I called Big Eddie and informed him I wasn't coming home for Thanksgiving, and that was painful because I didn't see him or my daughter for months. Then around December 20, my first sergeant informed me that since the majority of soldiers were taking leave and I hadn't gotten into any trouble, he was letting me go on leave (that moment played a huge part with Chris and me getting back together). I told Big Eddie that I was coming back for a week. I arrived in Brooklyn on December 22 with new gear, gold on my wrist, a gold chain, and driving my own car. For the first two days, I spent time with Big Eddie, my daughter and mostly Powerful, but during that whole week, a few of my former girlfriends visited and spent time with me. Big Eddie liked them but never was impressed by them. Powerful informed his mother I was in Brooklyn for a few days, and she informed Chris, who was already in Brooklyn for her college Christmas break.

The next day around 2:00 p.m., we talked on the phone, and she stated she was going out later that night with one of her longtime friends, Ebony B., and I told her I would be hanging out with Powerful. On December 24, I told Chris I would come by to see her that night. I played it cool and told her that I would come by around 9:00 p.m., but deep down inside I was like "Hell yeah." Powerful and I went to his apartment, and I saw Chris for the first time since the Greek Picnic the year before. We talked for an hour, then we left and went to Big Eddie's, and I introduced her to my daughter who was six months old. Big Eddie was excited that I was with Chris because he always liked her. Chris later told me she prayed to *God* to send her a good man to love her, and I believe Big Eddie probably prayed to *God* for a good woman to enter my life. Big Eddie pulled me aside and said, "Christine told me that if you ask her to marry you, she would say yes in a heartbeat. No bullshitting." I said to him that I would ask her. So later that night I asked her to marry me, and she said yes, and around 2:00 a.m. I took her back to her parents' apartment. The crazy part is if Big Eddie never told me that, Chris and I probably would have never married. I knew she was still in college and living in Philadelphia, and I was a soldier stationed near Savannah, and I never believed in long-distance relationships. Our intentions were just to meet, catch up, and maybe spend a lot of time together for a few days, since we both were missing something in the relationships, we were in. The

Lord and *Jesus Christ* must have been tired of us playing around and blessed Big Eddie to assist with getting us to be together.

On New Year's Day, we went to breakfast, and we talked out our plans for a wedding, then we left. We realized Big Eddie had manufactured the whole thing (which turned out great for us) because he had asked her if I would ask her to marry me what she would say, and she had stated she would say yes (she was thinking years later). I returned to base, and I informed my closest friends and my chief that I was engaged. Chris and I talked a lot on the phone during the first week of January 2000, then for Dr. Martin Luther King Jr.'s birthday, I had a four-day weekend (that meant I was off from working Friday through Monday), so after I got off from work that Thursday evening, I called her and stated I was driving to Philly to visit her for three days. Around 12:00 a.m. I felt sleepy, and I pulled over and slept in the back of my car in a hotel parking lot. I did not have a cell phone, so I couldn't call her. Chris was worried because she didn't hear from me, but I made it to her around 9:00 a.m. Friday morning. We spent three days enjoying being together, and I never worried about any of her former boyfriends approaching me because I was prepared if they did, and thanks to *God* and *Jesus Christ* none of them ever did.

When I returned to work the following Tuesday, my chief asked if I got married, and I told him I didn't, and he stated, "Private! I thought you got married already. I'm going to get first sergeant to give you a few days next month, so you can go back to Philly and marry your girl." So that night I talked with Chris, we set our marriage date for February 18, and we agreed not to tell anyone until after we were married. I arrived in Philly that weekend, and on Monday we went to the courthouse and paid for our marriage license and completed the other paperwork we needed to get married. Most importantly, we needed a witness, and we couldn't find any of our closest family members or friends to be one, so Chris asked Ebony C. (her friend from Temple) and she agreed, but she had a "this marriage is not going to last" facial expression. As a side note, we have been friends with Ebony C. for more than twenty years, and every time I see her, I remind her about her facial expression.

On the morning of February 18, I was excited and couldn't wait to marry Chris, and there was a snowstorm with at least half a foot of snow; nonetheless, in the afternoon, we picked up Ebony C. from her apartment, and we headed to the wedding chapel. We didn't have any money to purchase a bridal dress or rent a tuxedo, so Chris wore her high school prom dress and I wore my army class-A uniform (looks like a green suit). The chapel was located on the first floor of a row house, it was nice and warm inside, and a reverend married us within an hour. I carried Chris over the snow, into the car, we dropped Ebony C. off at her apartment, and we went back to Chris's apartment. I called Big Eddie and told him that we just got married, and he and Eleanor sent us fifty dollars as a congratulations gift because after we paid for our marriage certificate, we only had fifty cents to our names.

Starting Together in Georgia
(2000–2005)—Eddie's POV

The morning of February 19, 2000 was great but confusing. We were finally living out our dream of being married but were not quite sure what we would do next especially since I had to go back to Georgia in a few days. We barely knew anything about each other regarding the last four years, and if there was a class that taught the dos and don'ts of a marriage, we couldn't afford to attend it. After Big Eddie and Eleanor sent us money, we were left with twenty dollars for food for a few days, and we went to the supermarket. While we were in the frozen section, I grabbed her on her right hip, pulled her in tight, and started kissing her on her cheek (picture Pepé Le Pew). Chris pushed me away and stated, "I don't like this. I don't like showing public affection." That turned me off, and I was angry because I was one of those guys who wanted to show PDA since I learned that from Chad. He always showed his girlfriends PDA no matter if they were pretty or pretty ugly.

Chris and I were going to Ebony C.'s apartment that night for a game night, and since I was mad at Chris and didn't say anything to her, she asked me what was wrong, and I told her. I stated, "Chris. I'm the type of man who needs to

117

show the world that I'm in love with you, and if I can't do that, we probably won't make it. I want a divorce." She said, "Eddie, I love you, but I can't do that in public. I'm a lady." We made up and went to the game night, and everyone there was in college or was a college graduate, and even though all were down to earth, I felt intimidated, but I didn't let Chris know that until years later after I received my bachelor's degree. I left Philly early Sunday morning and returned to base, and in April, for the first time in her life, Chris came to Georgia and attended my Army Battery Ball, and she stayed for three days. I was living in the barracks with two roommates, and so I rented us a hotel room on base, and we enjoyed ourselves, then she returned to Philly, and I didn't get to see her again until she had her summer break.

I told my friends in the army and my closest friends in Brooklyn that I had married Chris; however, she on the other hand did not tell anyone except Natasha and Ebony B. and her friends at Temple. Therefore, Chris's parents found out the hard way. I was in the field training for two weeks, and around the twelfth day, that night I called Chris, and she was upset with her parents. I said, "Hello, love." She said, "Eddie! Guess what happened? My parents found out that we got married, and my father is pissed!" I said, "I told you to tell them." She said, "I know, but it would have broken my father's heart that he couldn't give me a wedding and walk me down the aisle." I asked her how they found out, and she said, "I was at my parents' house in my room sitting on my bed looking at the wedding pictures, and I left them on the bed and walked away. Next thing I knew my father said to me, 'Chris! What are these pictures? Did you and Eddie get married?' After I told him yes, it became a big thing since he told my mother and she told my grandmother." I told Chris, as hurtful as it may have been to all (including Big Eddie), Chris and I did what was best for us. We loved each other, and even though we planned to be married in a year, in reality it wouldn't have been our time because our time was February 2000. We married because we didn't want to lose each other again, and we didn't want to depend on having money to get married. Yes, we needed money for the marriage license, certificate, and the rings, but if we would have waited, we would have messed up our destiny.

In May I rented us a very nice two-story townhome in a quiet neighborhood ten minutes from base. Chris came for the summer and we were broke. I remember our neighbors' parents (who were veterans) gave us four single mattresses, and we pushed them together and made our first bed. We used bed sheets as curtains for a few weeks, and we had a small television that sat on two milk crates. I remember when we pulled every penny, we could find just to buy something to eat. At the end of the summer, Chris went back to college, and we didn't see each other again until September and then when she returned for Thanksgiving. In October 2000, I was deployed and spent a whole month in the desert in California (my second time), and then for Thanksgiving, Chris, Big Eddie, Eleanor, and my daughter came to Georgia when Chris was around six months pregnant, and we also had our neighbors Bus, his wife, and young son over. From the beginning, Bus respectfully talked about outdrinking my father, and by the end of the night, Bus was on the ground and had to be helped home (he was throwing up for two days). Big Eddie and I laughed at him, and his wife yelled at my father, saying, "Mr. Sledge! You're the devil." We all enjoyed ourselves for a few days, then Big Eddie, my daughter, and Eleanor went back to Brooklyn, and Chris stayed with me in Georgia.

We went back to Brooklyn for Christmas, and while there we ran into Tiffany from high school, who had connected us eight years earlier on that same block outside of the train station. It was serendipity! She was so happy to see that we got married and that we were expecting our first child together. Chris gave birth to our daughter Tiffany in March of 2001, one year after Mama passed away. She named Tiffany's middle name after Mama. We were elated that Tiffany was born. A few months later my daughter came to live with us. There was pressure placed on Chris to raise a child as her own at the age of twenty-three, also within a few months of our marriage and her pregnancy. It definitely was a lot to ask of her since she had already accepted the fact that the custody arrangement was complicated, and no one was supportive because they didn't instantly have a bond.

I also had a short temper with a "just keep pushing through" attitude, and Chris had a calm temperament that took time to explode and a "look at me and let's talk" attitude. I remember I used to throw and break things such as a laptop or printer just to make her stop talking, and she started to curse to defend herself. I was a hot-tempered man who cursed, and she was quiet and non-confrontational but stood up for herself, and that meant when we bumped heads neither of us was backing away. However, we made sure we always slept in the same bed at night. I was angry because of some of the people I had to put up with in the army, and also Chris wasn't backing down from me cursing and yelling. Both Chris and I have witnessed our parents' arguments, and those moments became embedded in us, plus we really didn't know each other's explode buttons yet. Ironically, those times made us stronger when they should have divided us. Since Chris was pregnant while in her last semester in college, she had to delay her final class to graduate, and she later finished that class at Savannah State University as a transient student. Chris graduated in the spring of 2002. Chris went to Temple on a Greyhound bus from Hinesville, Georgia, by herself to pick up her diploma and came right back, missing her graduation ceremony to get back home to us.

We had growing pains during our first two years of marriage since we were still getting to know each other. Our marriage changed for the better once Chris got a good-paying job located right outside of Savannah, and that was the jump we needed to start climbing upward. Thanks to *God* and *Jesus Christ*, we never looked back.

In the fall of 2000, I started having unexplainable terrifying and vivid dreams and I reported them to my chain of command. They sent me to the mental health clinic, and then to a sleep center and I was diagnosed with Narcolepsy. That meant I would have to take medicine for the rest of my life, and I was scheduled to be medically discharged from the army. I wasn't worried about life after the military regarding getting a job, but for almost a year, I didn't receive a solid discharge date. Not having a discharge date was extremely difficult for us because we were ready to start a new life outside the army, but we didn't know when. My commanders placed me on the staff duty roster list, and it consisted of a rotation of soldiers from battalion units working at the main desk at our headquarters. Every shift had two soldiers and a sergeant taking care of phone calls, situations, and cleaning the area within a twenty-four hour span. All three would have the next day off then report back to their respective units; however, the soldiers who were being discharged had permanent staff duty and didn't have to report back to their units.

Another life-changing moment for me was on October 31, 2001. I was on staff duty and instead of being at the front desk, the sergeant on duty told me to take a break; therefore, I went inside the conference room to watch television. At first, I was watching the late innings of game four of the 2001 World Series while the New York Yankees played the Arizona Diamondbacks (the Derek Jeter's Mr. November game). For some reason, I turned from the game, and I flipped through the channels and I started watching HBO's Def Poetry Jam (a spin-off of HBO's Def Comedy Jam). Def Poetry Jam was a poetry show that displayed established and upcoming poets. I never liked poetry; however, on that particular night and at that particular moment, I watched it. Nikki Giovanni was on stage speaking and I was stuck to the television while she called names of African Americans who lived and died during the civil rights era. It was crazy for me because I didn't know many of those names, and in those minutes, she spoke, my life changed. Those minutes prompted me to look for a deeper purpose in my life. To this day, I don't remember anything she said, but if she never believes that she made a difference in someone's life, she can believe she made a difference in my life (I told her that when I met h

Starting Together in Georgia
(2000–2005) Christina's
POV

The morning of February 19, 2000, the day after our wedding ceremony, was surreal. We had one more day together before Eddie drove back to Georgia. Our first argument as a married couple happened right there in the middle of a supermarket called Brown's Thriftway in North Philly. It was over Eddie wanting to be extremely intimate in the middle of the store. I was not comfortable with it and told him I loved him, but I was a lady, an introvert and didn't like flaunting our PDAs in front of everyone. He immediately said this was not going to work because that's the way he expressed his love. We learned years later that Eddie's love language is showing affection/touching, while my love languages are equally acts of service, showing appreciation, and quality time. We made up and went to the game night that was hosted by Ebony C., and our classmates from Temple were there. We played Taboo, and it was the guys against the girls. I knew Eddie was nervous, but he actually fit right in with the guys. Eddie left Philly early Sunday morning and returned to Georgia. I was not scheduled to see Eddie again until March for my birthday. I went to Brooklyn for spring break.

While there, my parents found out that we got married by finding the pictures of the ceremony, and my father and mother were pissed! We married because we didn't want to lose each other again, and we didn't want to depend on having money before we could finally get married. I explained to my parents that we married each other because we felt it was our destiny. Mama was understanding. She wished she could have witnessed it and met Eddie but understood. She was happy for me and prayed for our union. It was the last time I saw Mama. Mama's breast cancer returned, and it hurt all of us especially me since Mama was my rock. She always encouraged me to stay in school and pray for guidance from the Lord especially when times were rough. She always gave me hope. About a week later, after I got back from spring break, Mama passed away from cancer. I remember the night she died vividly. I was on my way home from school, walking home that night from the train station. While I was walking, an eerie feeling came over me like something bad happened. As soon as I reached my apartment, the phone was ringing, it was my grandmother telling me Mama passed away. My heart sank, and I didn't do well on my midterms because I was distracted by Mama's death. I was devastated by her death since she was such a driving force in my life. I believe Mama was at peace because she knew I was married and would not have to struggle by myself anymore. I lost Mama and gained Eddie at the right moment when I needed him. It was my new marriage to Eddie that helped me through losing Mama.

It was a pleasant distraction. Without him, I think I would have gone into a deep depression. I went to New York for Mama's funeral. When I got back to Philly, I had a terrible stomach virus right before my birthday. I was planning to visit Eddie in Georgia and had to get better, but I had no energy to even go to the store to get soup, crackers, or Gatorade. I was extremely dehydrated. I called all my friends, but I couldn't get a hold of anyone that could make it over to me. Trey was the only person I knew with a car to assist me. He bought me the soup, water, ginger ale, crackers, and Gatorade to get my fluids up. It was a risky decision because I was a married woman now. Eddie was pissed with me for calling Trey. I told him that I had no choice, and everything was above-board. We argued about it, but he was happy that I felt better. I was nursed back to health and went to visit Eddie in Georgia. I was excited since it was my first time going to the south. It was my birthday but also Eddie's army ball. We went on our first official date as husband and wife for my birthday in Savannah. We had a great trip and a welcome change that I needed.

In May, Eddie rented us a two-story townhome in a quiet neighborhood in Hinesville, Georgia, right outside of Ft. Stewart. When I visited for the summer, we were so broke that we had to scrape together money for food until the army basic allowance for housing (BAH) and food allowance kicked in. It was during that summer that I became pregnant with our daughter Tiffany. Here we were an instant family. I was an immediate stepmom. I had no idea what I was doing. I didn't know how to be someone else's mother let alone my own unborn child's mother yet. I struggled with emotions and never imagined how difficult it would be.

I visited Eddie a few times in my senior year fall semester while I was pregnant. I lived with my friend Ebony C. because she generously allowed me to sleep on her couch for four months. I had to move out of my apartment in Philly because I couldn't pay the rent and was being evicted. The BAH only covered enough for one rent. I am so grateful for Ebony until this day. It was rough being pregnant in my first two trimesters while being away from Eddie. I suffered from terrible morning sickness for four months but still had to go to school and worked part-time in the computer lab at Temple. Ebony lived in South Jersey, so I would commute in with her to Temple each day while she worked in Philly. I met up with her most days after work and school, and we commuted back to Jersey each night. I had my initial doctor visits in Philly, but they were at clinics with hordes of patients. I had to wait hours to see a doctor. That was not an ideal situation for my first pregnancy.

For Thanksgiving we planned for Big Eddie and Eleanor to travel to Georgia to spend it with me and Eddie. I was six months pregnant and decided I wouldn't go back to Temple to complete my finals to then have to travel back to Georgia in two weeks. I was getting farther along in my pregnancy and needed prenatal care more consistently at the army hospital. I arranged with my professors to finalize my grades since I completed all my final assignments before Thanksgiving, but one class needed a final exam, and I couldn't make it back up there, so I took an incomplete grade. This allowed me to finish that last class as a transient student in Savannah. We went back to Brooklyn for Christmas, and while there we ran into Tiffany from high school, who had connected us eight years earlier on that same block outside of the train station. It was fate! She was so happy to see that we got married and that we were expecting our first child together. It felt so surreal because we always talked about getting married, and to see Tiffany made our union come full circle.

I gave birth to our daughter, Tiffany (named after Tiffany who brought us together) in March of 2001. One year after Mama passed away. We were elated that Tiffany was born. She came into this world through an emergency C-Section. She was so long that she had limited room in my uterus. The umbilical cord was in knots. They delivered her and she was 8lbs, 5 oz. We were so blessed that she was born healthy especially after the ways Eddie and I came into this world. Within four weeks after Tiffany was born, we had to prepare for Eddie to go to a field exercise for two weeks. Which meant I would be without a car with a newborn for two weeks. By sheer will- power and determination, Eddie taught me to drive in those four weeks after I was cleared to drive by my doctor. Being from Brooklyn, we didn't need to learn to drive right away because we had public transportation. However, in Georgia it was a necessity. We also had one other hurdle to overcome which was my birth certificate didn't have my name on it. You may be scratching your head about this.

In NYC, for many decades if parents didn't name their babies while in the hospital, the gender of the baby and the mother's last name were listed as the first and last name of the newborn. Until I was twenty-three years old, my name on my birth certificate was "Female Hill". Eddie and I had to hire an attorney to get my name legally changed to my maiden name. Yes, my maiden name because I was now married. That meant when I went to get my driver's license, I had to bring my birth certificate, my legal name change document, and my marriage license. Within those four weeks of giving birth, I got my legal name change, learned to drive (including parallel parking between two of our kitchen chairs), and got my driver's license. The overachiever strikes again! I got my driver's license just in the nick of time on the day before Eddie left for the field. I had to drive our neighbor's Toyota Corolla because Eddie's New Yorker was difficult for me to maneuver while parallel parking.

Those first two years were rough as we experienced growing pains as husband and wife, parents and working parents. I eventually got an interview at a chemical plant. The job was located an hour away from our home. Eddie's car was in the shop for his transmission when they called me for the interview. We had to rent a car for $30 a day, which was disgusting and filthy inside. It paid off and within a few days they called to offer me the job! There were two catches, I was required to be on call twenty-four hours a day, and I was the only and first woman of color working there as a manager. It was a huge culture shock coming from a diverse world in NYC and Philadelphia to a very homogenous place in Savannah. I was ill prepared and ill equipped for the emotional toll it would take on me. I was miserable there. I was surrounded by confederate flags and people that never worked with a woman of color before. I witnessed one coworker say, "Oh did you hear they hired a black girl to work here?" I had to grin and take it and in a true Chris and Aries nature, I rose to the top and became a star employee. I also had a horrible boss that caused me to really dislike my job more. Although I did not like working there, I enjoyed accomplishment. I thrived on it. My Plant Manager

Rick began to mentor me and teach me how to thrive in that male dominated environment. I had to learn how to roll with the boys while not losing myself in the process. I went to lunch with them and spent time with them outside of work by attending social functions that I was invited to.

I became more assertive. I started a Diversity Council at our location to educate employees on diversity and the benefits to the workforce. I also became a member of the local elementary school's business community committee and volunteered at the school which had a predominately black student body. I represented my company at the school's career fair teaching students about careers in STEM. I prayed, read the bible, Essence, Black Enterprise, and a book by Iyanla Vanzant Faith in the Valley to get me through that tough time in my life. Eddie was also instrumental in teaching me how to toughen up. He taught me mind over matter, something he learned in the army. I learned work was business not personal, and to make lemonade out of lemons. I worked there for almost five years, and I grew stronger as a woman and leader because of that experience.

Throughout all of that, we had to deal with Eddie going to the field and as one of his duties in the army he worked twenty-four hour shifts, one day on and one day off. When September 11, 2001 happened, I was scared he would be deployed.

Also, I was ill-prepared for the struggles of being an army wife. It was expected that the soldier's career came first, and the army wife's work or career had to take a back seat. I didn't work so hard for my career to be insignificant. It was rough because all of our plans took a back seat to the army's protocols and norms. Eddie was soon diagnosed with Narcolepsy, and I believe those twenty-four hour shifts caused it. As a soldier, you can't have a sleeping disorder, so they medically and honorably discharged him. It was a blessing in dis- guise because his unit went to Iraq not too long after that.

I finished my final class at Savannah State University, a HBCU as a transient student. I graduated from Temple in the spring of 2002. I went to Temple on a Greyhound bus by myself since we didn't want to travel with Tiffany. I headed to my academic advisor who helped with the transient-student process. She said, "So you finally graduated, Christina!" I was so happy and proud at that moment to have the diploma in my hand that I sat on a bench outside her office and just wept. I was finally a college graduate. After all those years of being an honor student, working hard, and getting good grades, this was it. It was anticlimactic because I didn't attend the ceremony. I then got right back on the bus and went back home to Georgia. We moved to Savannah when Eddie was discharged that summer of 2002. Eddie immediately enrolled in Armstrong Atlantic

University (now Georgia Southern University) in Savannah using his GI Bill benefits. He worked at night at a TV station, and during the day he went to school. He grew so much in that time and learned so much that I could see his metamorphosis. He finished his degree in three and a half years. I was so proud of him!

In November of 2005, while Eddie was a few weeks from finishing his degree, I moved to Maryland and waited for him to join me. My godmother Shamean and her husband David generously allowed me to stay with them for three weeks until our apartment was ready. Eddie graduated college, and we moved into our apartment in December of 2005. I felt a sigh of relief and instantly had a sense of joy moving from Georgia to Maryland.

Part Three: Love and Marriage

Our Marriage Philosophy

We decided after getting married that we were in this marriage together and we wanted to honor our wedding vows, especially since we married each other three separate times. We renewed our wedding vows twice, once at fifteen years and again at twenty years. Each time served as recommitment celebrations for those big milestones. We don't live in drama or negativity. Do we have disagreements and arguments? Yes, we do. It took us years to learn how to communicate with each other during an argument, so we didn't regret our words. We now pick our battles wisely. If we find the argument isn't worth it, we just drop it. Other times there are screaming matches, but they are now few and far between. We much rather love on each other than fight with each other. We also don't let arguments fester. We much rather tackle it and move on. We decided to focus our energy on our children and our goals. From 2000 until year twenty-one, we set short term and long-term goals for ourselves every year. Whether it was another degree, writing this book, a new endeavor, a 5K race, a new job, vacation, or losing weight.

We made it our focus to accomplish our goals. We knew that setting our intention for our lives together would provide us with a roadmap for success. Not only do we set goals, but we also set forth a plan of action to accomplish our goals. We always write them down and make them specific and time bound. We always go in with a positive attitude and a growth mindset. We are not afraid to take calculated risks in the name of progress. We also support and encourage each other while working on our goals. We planned out our lives together in the early years, when we would obtain our degrees, when would purchase a house, where we saw our careers and lives in five years, ten years, and twenty years. We set milestones and chipped away bit by bit on our goals. After we accomplished one goal, we set another goal. We also believe in manifestation and the law of attraction.

We learned over time that patience is key, and hiccups happen, but we decided perseverance and prayer would be our guiding lights. We also keep our goals private until we accomplish them. We believe that practice keeps us resolute. We thrive on accomplishment and teach our children to do the same. We work really hard and we play hard. We enjoy working hard to be able to provide for our family. We also enjoy entertainment and fun times. We frequently spend our weekends taking the children to vacations, amusement parks, unique attractions like indoor skydiving and virtual reality experiences, museums, zoos, parks, and escape rooms, playing board games, and watching movies and documentaries together.

We learned parenting takes patience, commitment, and understanding. It also includes surprises, protection, courage, moments, forgiveness, and love. When our youngest daughter, Olena was born in 2008, and we learned how to juggle two children, full-time jobs, and a household. Balancing work and our family were challenging in the beginning for us, and we learned through trial and error just like other parents. As parents, we had to learn quickly as young adults how to be resilient and to be supportive. We made it our priority to instill in our daughters the importance of education and the importance of giving and receiving respect. We also equipped them with the ability to be resourceful and to figure out the situation they faced or can face in their futures. We are proud of our children, and we are extremely proud of who they are becoming.

When obstacles come our way, we dust ourselves off and keep moving. When more than one obstacle comes in our path, we just tackle each one at a time. We realized early on that if we could survive both of us being unemployed at the same time, we could survive anything. We believe our New York toughness prepared us for anything. We are driven to succeed. We rely on each other and our faith in *God* to get us where we need to be. We like to learn from our mistakes and use those mistakes to propel us.

Eddie has this cute tradition he does with the girls and me. When he finds a new food product in the grocery store like potato chips or ice cream, he brings it home for us all to try, and he screams "Taste test!" and we all come running into the kitchen to try it. That is an ode to Lacee Griffith from the morning news here in Maryland on WBAL-TV. It is a testament to how far he has come from not always having dinner to eat as a child to now buying a brand new product just for us to try. Just for our happiness and enjoyment. We laugh every day and focus on the positive moments in our day more than the difficult ones. We choose to focus on things that make us happy and bring us joy and laughter. We are content with just staying home and enjoying each other's time and company. On Sundays we take it easy like the Commodores and just wake up late, have brunch, and watch the news and football during football season or Super Soul Sunday.

We are grateful to be here and remember the tough times. We have been blessed, and we are extremely grateful for our blessings and opportunities.

THE STORY OF CHRISTINA AND I

Our Experience with Deaths

Sadly, during our twenty-one years of marriage, we have endured several deaths from both sides of our friends and families, and this chapter discusses the lost ones who touched us profoundly. The first death we experienced was Mama's. She died on March 20, 2000, a month, and two days into our marriage. Mama was Chris's heart and rock (Mama was to so many) because she was there when Chris needed someone to count on and words of encouragement. Chris found out shortly before Mama died that her breast cancer had returned, but because Chris was in college, she could not be there for Mama as much as she wanted to. Mama taught Chris how to be the woman she is today. The twenty-two years Chris was blessed to have Mama in her life made a profound impact. Mama and her family lived through the Great Depression, and Mama believed that brought her close-knit family closer together. Mama was the last surviving sibling of her five siblings. Chris remembers Mama's confidence and her contentment with her life. She reminisces and honors Mama daily, from the way Chris makes French toast to the way she makes her pot roast and when she watches *60 Minutes* the way

Mama used to. Chris values the time they spent together and misses her dearly.

A year and four months later, Big Eddie complained about having back pains. He was placed in a wheelchair because he was diagnosed with cancer. He was then hospitalized, and thankfully, Eddie was granted two days of family leave to see him. The first night Eddie saw him, he had an oxygen mask on and was awake, and they talked to each other for close to an hour, and then the next morning on August 8, 2001, Eddie saw him before Eddie returned to Georgia, and Big Eddie died that night. Eddie's father wasn't the greatest man, but he became the greatest man in Eddie's life. Big Eddie influenced all who knew him since he was a poor single father on welfare who loved his women, liquor, family, parties, and especially his son Eddie. He was Eddie's rock and his world since he taught Eddie about life and most importantly about having patience because at that time, he understood Eddie was a young man who did not have patience. When Eddie was around ten years old, his father visited the doctor for chest pains, and the doctor told him if he smoked another cigarette, his lungs will collapse and he will die, so after thirty-plus years of smoking, he stopped smoking that day. Eddie truly believes the cancer didn't kill him, but the loneliness did. Before Eddie left for the army, Big Eddie's apartment had his friends and family, they drank and partied, but that changed after Eddie left. Pete went into a drug rehab center, and Big Eddie became extremely lonely.

We both planned Big Eddie's funeral arrangements, and after he died, Eddie's attitude about life changed because Eddie just wanted to be alone and changed his phone number. He only kept in touch with his closest friends. Eddie now understands why his father was an alcoholic. Big Eddie witnessed so much heartache and so many terrible events that Eddie thought he enjoyed drinking; however, it never occurred to him that Big Eddie was self-soothing and drinking away his pain. Big Eddie witnessed a lynching, traveled from Tennessee to New York by himself as a teenager, witnessed both loves of his life die, and had his best friend who was his youngest son, leave him to join the army.

In the winter of 2010, Chris received a phone call from her brother Brandon and was told that her closest cousin, Kena, was found dead by her husband at home; she had taken her own life. Her death shocked all who knew her because she was an extremely well-loved and intelligent pediatrician. She and Chris grew up together in the same building and were the same age. Kena's death really devastated Chris. She thought they would grow old together. Kena is dearly missed by Chris and her family.

In November 2012, we lost our first cat, Sophia, and she had lived with us for five years. Eddie always wanted a cat, and we agreed when we bought a house that we would get one; therefore, we went to Petco and adopted Sophia because the employee stated she was two years old. However, the day before she passed, she was barely breathing, and Eddie took her to the vet, and the vet said her heart was one of a cat twelve years old. The vet provided her medication, but we knew it was just a matter of time. The next day, our daughters told Eddie Sophia wasn't moving, and we rushed her to the vet. Eddie decided to put her to sleep since the vet recommended it. We loved her so much because she just wanted to be around us all the time. She was a happy and loved cat, and when she died, it hit us hard because she was deeply part of our family especially because our daughters grew up with her.

On Thursday, November 3, 2016, around 1:00 p.m. Powerful was shot while leaving a laundromat with his girlfriend a few blocks from where they lived. We went straight to the hospital, and we saw his girlfriend and a few of Powerful's Five Percenter brothers in the waiting room. She told us some guys came inside the laundromat and were talking to Powerful, and the guys left before she and Powerful did. A few young guys were across the street, and they called Powerful to come over, and while he crossed the street, someone came behind him and shot him twice in the back of the head and once in the neck. After hearing the shots, she turned around and saw Powerful on the ground bleeding, and she grabbed a bedsheet and wrapped it around his head and screamed for help. His parents and Brianna made it down to the hospital around 7:00 p.m., and then they, his girlfriend, and both of us sat in a cold room around a table.

Two doctors came in and informed us the seriousness of the wounds and that he would be brain dead and living on life support. For five days, Chris's parents, friends, and family visited him, and on Tuesday, November 8, 2016, he was pronounced dead. Through the last day, Chris took an emotional toll from being the next of kin proxy when the doctor called requesting permission to give Powerful a blood transfusion and also when they called when he went into cardiac arrest. Chris was so strong to plan for the funeral while her family grieved. She is the type of person that goes into action to get things done, and that is what she did to help her family. It finally hit her after the funeral. Chris had to go to grief counseling for months to deal with her brother's death. She internalized the grief and stopped working out. She gained twenty pounds in four months. She really struggled with Powerful's passing. She vowed to get justice for his death.

After we got married, Powerful saw us in Savannah, then he lived with us in Maryland for a few weeks before he brought his girlfriend and three kids from Brooklyn to Maryland to live a better life. In late 2006, Eddie got him a job working with him, and all the employees and Eddie's employer loved him because he completed jobs three times faster than the average employee. Two months later Powerful got into a car accident while in Brooklyn and hurt his back, then he quit his job. That caused a ripple effect of unfortunate events in his life. In April 2019, two and a half years after Powerful's murder, Chris, her parents, her godfather, Tiffany, and Brandon arrived at the courthouse to witness the sentencing of one of the four murder suspects. Months before that moment, Chris had become extremely involved in the process of seeking justice. We went to see the Assistant District Attorney (ADA) and the lead detective with pictures sharing that Powerful was a young man raised by a tight-knit loving family who just took wrong turns in life. That moment was extremely critical, and the ADA and detective worked tirelessly to arrest the suspects; however, the cops could not directly connect two of the suspects to the crime. It was definitely an unimaginable experience for all of us, one that we never thought we would live through.

At the sentencing, the scene felt surreal and definitely not what we saw on television. It was more in-depth, extremely quiet, and sobering. The suspect was a twenty-seven year old black male with a criminal record. We sat in the courtroom, and he came out with two prison guards, and he was wearing a yellow prison jumpsuit with his feet and hands in chains. He looked straight at us while we sat in the rows directly behind him, and then he sat in his chair with large bold black letters "DOC" on his back. After opening arguments by the suspect's lawyer and then the ADA, who asked the judge to sentence the suspect to life without parole, Chris walked and stood on the left side of the ADA and read her and her mother's statements. In the middle of Chris's statement while she was crying, Eddie walked up to her and stood with her for support. At that time, their godfather Rolando and a few of Powerful's closest friends arrived, and we sat down. The judge informed the suspect to rise and asked him if he had anything to say to the court, and he quietly stated no and shook his head while looking down. Then the judge sentenced him and without banging a gavel or even stating anything else, the judge stood up and walked away. The suspect walked with the guards back through the door they came from. We stood there wondering what was next, then another case was called, and we all hugged each other and left.

We endured another unfortunate death in January 2018, when Chris's grandmother Ellen died at the age of seventy-two from cardiac arrest. She was an intelligent and beautiful woman who wasn't afraid to speak her mind since she went through a lot in her life. It was another death that was difficult for her family to come to grips with.

In October 2018, we lost our second cat, Melo, to asthma, and again that was an extremely heart-breaking time for us. On February 14, 2013, we adopted Melo when we drove through two feet of snow to Petco (the same store where we adopted Sophia). He was a stray cat from the streets, and he looked like he had a rough life as one of his ears was nipped at the top point like a pit bull's ear. Petco told us he was a two-year-old female, so for the first couple of days, we gave him female names and even a female collar; however, one day Eddie was playing with him and noticed he wasn't a female, and Eddie knew Petco definitely got it wrong, again. We all took to Melo instantly, and we all cared for him because he brought us joy and laughter. He was especially picky with his food, loved his treats, and loved when Eddie gave him belly kisses / raspberries (at least we thought he did).

The night he passed away, Olena and Eddie were playing with him, then around 10:00 p.m. she stated he was on the ground and not moving. Eddie went to see him, and he was laying on his side with his eyes open, lifeless, and trying to catch his breath, and Eddie knew automatically he wasn't going to make it through the night because that was how Sophia looked before she died. Tiffany and Eddie took him to the emergency vet hospital, and one of the vets stated Melo was in a critical stage and probably would not make it through the night. He had an asthma attack, and

147

his lungs were full of fluid, and he probably had heart disease. The vet placed Melo into an oxygen-filled cage and told us we should call anyone who wanted to see him for the last time; therefore, Eddie called Chris, and she and Olena arrived in fifteen minutes to see Melo. He became worse in the cage, running around gasping for air, and for a few seconds, Melo looked at Eddie in his eyes because he recognized him, and Eddie told him he loved Melo over and over. Melo was foaming out of his mouth and looked as to say, "I love you, too." After Olena talked to him, he started panicking, and the vet told us we had to go because Melo was about to die. However, Eddie gave the OK to put Melo to sleep because he was suffering. Once the vet took him out of the oxygen cage, Melo died in his arms, and we all cried, and to this day when we speak about Melo we use caution because of the fear that talking too much about him will make us break down.

In June 2019, Chris found out from her mother that Chris's biological father, Jean, passed away from colon cancer. It came as a shock because before that moment, we barely talked about him since Chris didn't have contact with him but sometimes just wanted to talk with him and inform him how successful she had become. Chris has a higher risk of colon cancer since her biological father died of it. She received her first colonoscopy at forty-one years old to ensure she is proactive in preventing it. In 2021, Chris connected with Jean's family, which included her cousin, aunts, and siblings. Chris also connected with her sister Kadriene. Chris was extremely excited to get to know her sister.

In September 2019, we lost Eddie's Uncle Clarence to a heart attack. He was sixty-two years old and had high blood pressure. Ten years earlier he had passed out and was hospitalized for a whole month, and he never told Eddie. Around 10:00 a.m., he was at work and happy to be there especially since that was his fortieth anniversary working at the post office. He went to the bathroom, and after ten minutes he did not return, and one of his coworkers went to check on him and saw Clarence face down in his blood, dead. He had a heart attack, slipped, hit his head on the sink, busted his head open, and fell on the floor. Eddie's uncle witnessed Eddie turning from a young street kid into a strong husband and father, and he was so proud of Eddie and our family. Chris, Olena, and Eddie drove down to Virginia for his funeral, and it was a beautiful service, but Eddie didn't walk up to see him because he didn't want to see him in a casket; however, Eddie was one of the pallbearers. Uncle Clarence was extremely loved by his friends and family; all enjoyed his company and friendship since he was a good friend but even a greater man.

Through the pain of losing loved ones, we learned to be grateful for the time we spend with the people we love. We also learned that no one is promised tomorrow, so we learned to live our lives to the fullest. We decided to reach for all of our goals and accomplish everything we seek to do in life. We learned to seize the day and cherish our time here on earth by doing the things we love.

Memorable Moments & Achievements

One of the greatest moments we had as parents was when we took the girls to Universal Studios and to Disney World in 2013, and while we were at Walt Disney World, Chris set up a time for Olena to be dressed up as a princess at the Bibbidi Bobbidi Boutique. When we got there, Chris agreed to have Olena's hair done in the window by one of the Fairy Godmothers, so everyone would see her. All the little girls who were princesses lined up and walked in a princess parade through the neighborhood, and it was a very magical moment. Another great moment happened when Eddie took Tiffany and Olena to their first New York Giants football game at MetLife Stadium to watch the Giants play the Atlanta Falcons. They walked through the parking lot, and the girls were amazed to be around thousands of Giants fans, and that entire day was amazing especially because Eddie never thought he would be at a New York Giants game cheering with his daughters.

We had many memorable moments as parents in 2019, and one of those was when Tiffany received her driver's license. Assisting her with learning how to drive and receiving her license was one of our greatest achievements as parents. That entire process took a lot of patience and guidance

151

from us because we had to adjust our schedules and pay to make sure Tiffany received her license. When Chris got off from work, she had to take Tiffany to the required driving classes for two weeks straight, and Eddie picked her up after he had a long day of work. Then we created a schedule to teach her how to drive, which required Tiffany to have at least sixty hours driving. That was rough for us, but it was also rewarding. One morning Eddie let her drive him to the Red Cross to donate blood, and she pulled into an empty parking spot, and instead of slowing down she sped up and crashed into a concrete pillar. They were fine, and there were only a few scrapes on the front of Eddie's Lexus. Weeks later after she received her license, from our living room window we watched her get into Eddie's car, drive off, and return safely from the supermarket.

Another moment was buying Tiffany a car. Chris prearranged to have the salesman waiting for us, and Tiffany test drove a few cars until we bought her a car, and she has been driving ever since. For us, that was a moment we have always waited for because it was a sign of Tiffany's independence and a major accomplishment for us as parents. Another great moment as parents was when Chris and Tiffany in April 2019, went to the University of Maryland Baltimore County (UMBC) campus student day. Even though she was accepted to Eddie's alma mater, Towson University, it made sense from a financial and locational perspective for her to choose UMBC (an Honors' University). While they were sitting and hearing the school's president students talk about their experiences and their acceptance into graduate and PhD programs at universities such as Harvard and Oxford, Chris became overwhelmed with pride and joy that our daughter was accepted into UMBC. That moment, experiencing Tiffany being accepted to an honors university left Chris speechless.

From where we both came from; we have been blessed to attain four degrees between us. Chris is the first in her immediate family to have at least a bachelor's, and Eddie is the first in his entire family to have a bachelor's. Eddie entered undergrad in the fall of 2002, and his major was dentistry, but he changed it to history for three reasons. The first reason was Eddie's GI Bill benefits wouldn't pay more than thirty-six months, and dentistry would have taken longer than that. The second reason was we wanted to move from Georgia to Maryland no later than the end of 2005, and finally, Eddie loved history and wanted to tell people about it. Eddie was excited because he never received a college acceptance letter before, and he couldn't believe that just less than a year ago, he was scared to write a paper more than five pages long. Chris had a good-paying job, and Eddie used his GI Bill benefits to supplement the loss of his salary he used to receive in the army. Eddie really enjoyed and excelled at Armstrong Atlantic

State University (currently Georgia Southern University). He enrolled in five to six classes per spring and fall semester and at least four during summer semesters. He made the dean's list, received an award, presented several presentations in front of large groups of classmates, and wrote many papers more than five pages long, and he enjoyed writing them. Because Eddie was a nontraditional student (he was twenty-five years old), he had to take and pass a few remedial math and writing courses. Indeed, Eddie graduating college was one of our most memorable moments.

In October 2005, Chris accepted a job in Maryland, and a few weeks later, she moved and lived with her godmother Shamean and her husband David after Thanksgiving until Eddie graduated college. On December 9, three of Eddie's friends and their girlfriends drove from Brooklyn to see Eddie graduate while Chris was flying in from Maryland. Chris got off work late and had to take a late flight to Charlotte then to Savannah; however, she arrived in Charlotte on the last flight in and missed her connecting flight, and that was the last flight out that night. That meant that she would have to wait for a morning flight and miss Eddie's graduation, and if she wasn't there, Eddie was not going to walk across the stage especially since she turned down the opportunity to walk across the stage at her graduation ceremony at Temple University. So, one of Eddie's best friends, Rich and his girlfriend picked him up in his car around 9:00 p.m., and drove for four hours, picked up Chris at the airport, and drove back. We made it back an hour and a half before the graduation. They all left the next day, and we are still grateful for that.

Another memorable moment came in November 2006, when we bought our first home. Since Chris arrived in Maryland and started her new job, she quickly rented us a huge three-bedroom apartment located on the top floor in a great community. Five days later, after Eddie graduated, he and Tiffany packed up our house, and drove from Georgia to Maryland. Tiffany sat in the passenger seat, and with boxes between them, they couldn't see each other throughout most of the ride; it took them more than eleven hours to drive from the warm sunny south into the cold snowy north. In February 2006, Eddie found a job, and when his pay increased, we looked at several homes in the Columbia section of Howard County. At twenty-seven years old, we purchased our first home in November 2006. It was a three-story townhome with a fully finished basement in the quiet beautiful suburbs, and we loved it.

Another memorable moment was when Eddie received his master's degree. He attended graduate school at Towson University, and he excelled in his social science concentration courses. Eddie's goal was to graduate as fast as he could because he didn't want his funding from the VA to

CHRISTINA & EDWARD SLEDGE

run out, so he took three classes each semester (including summer). In order for him to graduate, he had to write a thesis. He wrote it regarding the media's participation in fueling three major American race riots, and he named it "The Birth of the Death of a Nation: 1917–1921, The Media's Role in Three Race Riots." Its goal is to show how the misreporting, negative stories, and images regarding African Americans provided by the media helped secure protection and social rights for whites. It explains the connection between whites' and African Americans' reactions to their environments, how customs and racist images contributed to violent reactions between the two races, and why the media continued to display those images. In December 2013, he walked across the stage for a second time.

Another memorable moment was in November 2013, when we went to a college basketball game between Temple University and Towson University. It was a very rare event that the schools played each other, especially at Towson, and Chris and Olena wore Temple shirts and sweaters, and Tiffany and Eddie wore Towson sweaters. It was a great moment for the family celebrating our schools and, in the process, sharing a college experience with our daughters. In the summer of 2014, Eddie came up with the idea to have a fifteenth wedding anniversary vow renewal. Throughout the years, we talked about having a wedding with all of our closest friends and family members. We started the planning process for our wedding scheduled for July 2015. We had our wedding, and it was beautiful because our friends and family were there. Fifty guests partied and enjoyed the moment with us.

In 2017, we decided that we wanted all of us to go on vacation to Toronto, Canada. We drove eight hours and crossed into Canada, and Chris drove to Toronto. We stayed at the four-star Hyatt Hotel on the Mink Mile, we ate at a nice restaurant, and around 8:00 p.m. we walked and took pictures in front of the famous Toronto sign. We took an Uber truck back to the hotel, and when we arrived in front of the hotel, Eddie saw New York Yankees pitchers Dellin Betances and CC Sabathia. Eddie jumped out and started talking (they were scared because he just jumped out on them), letting them know that we were Yankees fans who had come to see them play the next night. The next day, we did a Rogers Centre tour around the stadium, and that included sitting in the dugout and standing on the field, a real dream come true for Eddie. During the next two days, we visited a huge castle called the Casa Loma, went to a baseball game, went to the top of Canada's tallest building called the CN Tower, toured the city, and ate a lot of great food. On the way back to Maryland, we stopped at Niagara Falls on the Canada side, and Olena and Eddie did a boat ride around the horseshoe of the Falls, becoming soaking wet from their knees down. We all entered the upside-down house, and then before we headed back to Maryland, Tiffany and Eddie went into the Nightmares Fear Factory, and that was a terrifying experience.

In late May 2018, Chris's parents, Tiffany, Olena, and Eddie watched Chris graduate and receive her master's degree from George Washington University. Her parents, godmother Shamean and her husband David, godfather Rolando, and many friends came and celebrated Chris's graduation party with us in Maryland. It was a great celebration since Chris worked so hard, and again she planned and orchestrated the entire event because she's an event producer. A year later, another surreal moment occurred when she became a business owner, launching Christina's Confetti Events.

Conclusion

We were predestined to marry each other. Our love story is a testimony to follow your hearts and listen to *God*'s plan for your life. So how have we made it work for twenty-one years? We came into our marriage with hope and promise. We barely had any money, but we knew it would get better. We did not have any moments when we thought we wanted out of our marriage because we always knew we had a bright future. We have been blessed to live in beautiful, peaceful, and very comfortable communities. As a matter of fact, everywhere we have lived since we were married, we have always heard birds chirping in the morning. We also never did anything that was detrimental or something that would have hindered the positive flow of our marriage because we recognized that we must be on the same page to have progress. We faced several challenges that only required patience to overcome, and we never committed infidelity.

We trust and support each other to achieve goals. We have also had disappointments and more than a handful of heated and hurtful arguments. We had our share of issues, such as having narcolepsy, high blood pressure, gaining and losing weight, sinus infections, allergies, injuries, surgeries, and a mini stroke. We use social media mainly for business purposes, and our family business stays in our home. We embrace the moments we share, and we continue to seek peace and patience. We know and embrace who we are, and we are comfortable with it. We understand our roles, what we need to take care of, and take the necessary steps to move forward. We know the most important parts in our marriage are trust, love, communication, and patience.

As parents, we provide for our daughters and teach them to be respectful, helpful, and appreciative especially from the examples we display. We are careful with our words, but at the same time extremely direct explaining to them life situations and issues, and we are strict with them regarding education, paying attention to their surroundings, and of course boys. We display and explain to them the importance of an education, so they have chances to pursue and live their dreams. Since they were young, we exposed them to our undergraduate and graduate experiences.

They were right there for our long hours of writing papers, completing assignments to pass courses, the research and completion of Eddie's thesis, and Chris's long hours completing her practicum and grad school. As a matter of fact, Chris was pregnant with Tiffany while sitting in classes finishing her final semesters toward her bachelor's degree. Therefore, having both daughters graduate their respective grades (sixth and twelfth) the same year were proud moments for us. As parents, those graduations showed us we did an outstanding job leading our daughters on the right path of success. We also display our affection for one other, and our daughters know that through all tough times, their parents are still happily married.

We will end our book with a magical moment. Right before our twentieth anniversary, we had another vow renewal with our Disney Fairy Tale wedding. We talked about having a party to celebrate our twentieth anniversary, but we did that for our fifteenth anniversary, so we wanted something different. One day, Chris was watching episodes of the show Disney Fairy Tale Weddings, and Eddie told her they should do it, just the two of them at Christmastime because she always wanted to see Disney World during Christmastime. Also, she always wanted a Christmas wedding twenty years earlier when we were first engaged. She immediately looked into it, and after months of planning, on December 21, we took a direct flight from Maryland to Orlando. We stayed at the Coronado Springs Resort, then after we settled in, we went to Magic Kingdom to see a Christmas event at night, which Chris loved. The next day, we went to Hollywood Studios and Disney Springs, then on Monday, December 23, at noon we were picked up by a limo and taken to the site of our vow renewal at the Grand Floridian Resort. It was a great time for us because we were first married with one witness, and we celebrated the third time being married with just one witness, our wedding planner.

Moving toward another twenty-one years, we have plans for Chris to take her company to the next level, and she plans to publish an entertaining book. We plan on watching Eddie earn his doctorate and also witnessing our daughters graduate with their degrees. Hopefully we see parts of the world we always wanted to visit, speak at a TEDx, start a scholarship, mentor the next generation, and retire together. Ultimately, we hope everyone who reads our book enjoys and embraces our blessed stories and understands how we became the people we are now.

And they lived happily ever after...

THE END

About the Authors
Christina S. Sledge & Edward L. Sledge Jr.

Christina and Edward live in Maryland with their daughters. They have been happily married for more than 21 years. Born and raised in Brooklyn, NY, Christina received an undergraduate degree from Temple University and a graduate degree from The George Washington University. Edward received an undergraduate degree from Georgia Southern University and a graduate degree from Towson University. They started Sledge House Media in 2021. Both are planning to write more books together in the future.

For speaking engagements and to contact them: www.sledgehousemedia.com

Instagram: @sledgehousemedia

Twitter: Sledge House Media @house_sledge

CPSIA information can be obtained
at www.ICGtesting.com
Printed in the USA
LVHW022049160721
692932LV00009B/647